CHRIST AND KRISHNA

The Path of Pure Devotion

"In My Father's house there are many mansions."
—*John 14.2*

"I am the seed-giving Father of all living entities."
—*Bhagavad-gita 14.4*

Appreciations From
═══ Scholars, Ministers and Laymen ═══

"*Christ and Krishna* by Kirtanananda Swami Bhaktipada is a milestone in interreligious dialogue literature...The concern of the book is not sectarian propaganda but respiritualization of the world, devotion to God and a sane life."
—Dr. Klaus Klostermaier, *Professor of Religious Studies,*
  The University of Manitoba, Winnipeg, Canada

"*Christ and Krishna* is a masterpiece of comparative religious study...you have shown that the message of the Christian and the Vedic scriptures is the same."
—Rev. John T. Chewning, *Rector and Vicar of the*
  Episcopal Church, Fort Fairfield, Maine

"*Christ and Krishna* promises to bring a healing touch of reconciliation in interreligious relationships."
—K.L. Seshagiri Rao, *Professor of Religious Studies*
  University of Virginia

"If open-minded Christians listen to this and understand, I believe there could be full and total communion."
—Russell Edmunds, *Catholic Deacon, St. Mary's*
  Professor of History, Penrith Technical College, Australia

"This is an excellent book which is very useful in courses on new religions."
—Dr. Irving Hexham, *Dept. of Religious Studies*
  University of Calgary, Alberta, Canada

"A worthwhile addition to any spiritual library."
—New Age Teachings
  Brookfield, Mass.

"This knowledge should be taught in colleges...a wonderful book!"
—Sriman Karunakaran
  Chief Minister, State of Kerala, India

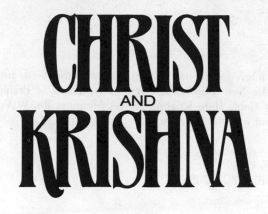

CHRIST
AND
KRISHNA

The Path of Pure Devotion

HIS DIVINE GRACE KĪRTANĀNANDA
SWAMI BHAKTIPĀDA

INTRODUCTION BY HARVEY COX

PALACE
PUBLISHING

Readers interested in the subject matter of this book are invited to visit the New Vrindaban Community, Home of Prabhupada's Palace of Gold, Hare Krishna Ridge, Moundsville, W.Va., or to correspond with the Secretary.

c/o New Vrindaban
R.D.1, Box 319
Moundsville, W.Va. 26041

First Printing 10,000 copies
Second Printing 50,000 copies
Third Printing 50,000 copies

© 1987 Palace Publishing
All Rights Reserved
Previous Edition © 1985 Bhaktipada Books

Printed in Singapore

Library of Congress Catalog Card No. 85-073024
ISBN: 0-932215-03-3

CONTENTS

BOOKS by
His Divine Grace
Kirtanananda Swami Bhaktipada

SONG OF GOD – A Summary Study of Bhagavad-gita As It Is
CHRIST AND KRISHNA – The Path of Pure Devotion
ETERNAL LOVE – Conversations with the Lord in the Heart
ON HIS ORDER
RAMA – The Supreme Personality of Godhead
LILA IN THE LAND OF ILLUSION
A PILGRIM'S PROGRESS TO THE SPIRITUAL SKY

A complete catalog is available upon request.

Palace Publishing
New Vrindaban Community
RD 1, Box 320
Moundsville, WV 26041

Author's Note
To The New Edition

Since this little book was published about a year and a half ago, we have been asked to talk about the messages of Christ and Krishna in many of the 50 U.S. cities on our 1987 First Amendment Freedom Tour. The response to *Christ and Krishna* has been quite overwhelming. Many individuals and groups have found the book's insights on interreligious harmony to be urgently relevant to their own spiritual lives, as well as to the problems of today's religious institutions.

For this new edition, Professor Harvey Cox, my long-time friend and a highly respected theologian, has written a very personal account of his own search to discover the relationship between Lord Jesus and Lord Krishna. This has not been an "armchair inquiry" for Dr. Cox, as he has visited Krishna's birthplace in India several times, and has addressed this subject in his comparative religion classes at Harvard for many years. I want to thank Dr. Cox for his beautiful Introduction, which is a brilliant essay in itself.

After a long search, I recently came across a 20-year-old letter to me from my beloved spiritual master, Srila Prabhupada, who originally requested me to write this book:

> "Because our movement is approved by Lord Jesus
> Christ, at least the Christian world will accept our
> *kirtan* (chanting and praising God's names) proce-
> dures. I have seen in the Bible that Lord Jesus
> Christ recommends this performance of *kirtan*. You
> know better than me, and I would request you to
> write a small book on this."   4/7/67

Many, many people have written to us expressing the joy they received from reading *Christ and Krishna*. I hope you experience it too.

Kirtanananda Swami Bhaktipada
April 7, 1987

i

Author's Note
To The New Edition

Harvey Cox

Each year countless devotees become pilgrims and wind their way to the sacred city of Vrindaban in India, the place of Krishna's pastimes. The city is full of temples, some occupying whole blocks, others more like modest storefronts. How many temples are there? Some say there are hundreds, others, thousands. In any case, in each one of them throngs of people offer praise to Lord Krishna every day of the year. The whole town seems to vibrate with the lilt of the great mantra.

When I first found myself in Vrindaban many years ago I visited all the temples I could, so many that at the end of the day I would often feel weary, though satisfied that I had seen so much beauty and devotion. One day, just before I left, a friend who is a devotee pointed out to me a tiny, wooden building by the side of the road and told me in warm tones that it was the chapel used by the first Christian who had ever come to live in Vrindaban, though it now no longer is in use. As a Christian myself, I felt drawn to this unlikely little temple, built and consecrated to the one I call "Lord." I walked over to it, ran my fingers along its walls and peeked in a window. I began to wonder. What did the prophet from Nazareth have to do with the midnight flute player? Was Christ Himself also somehow present here in a city where, as the saying goes, everyone—including the men—is a "gopi" (one of the cowherd girls who worshiped Krishna)?

Christ and Krishna. Krishna and Christ. What do these figures—perhaps the two most widely known and admired personalities in world history—have to do with each other? Is the relationship between the two one of petty jealousy, like that of the fractious gods and goddesses whose escapades we read of in the Greek tales and myths? Or, do they reign over something like "spheres of influence" with Christ representing God in the West and Krishna in the East? Are they two manifestations of the same divine reality, simply revealing its different aspects? Are they contending claimants to unique and exclusive devotion?

Somehow none of these standard answers satisfied me. I recognized that while I was in Vrindaban I had never once forgotten that I am a Christian. But I had at the same time felt the powerful fascination exercised by the winsome figure of Krishna. I had found myself entering enthusiastically into temple worship with its joyous music of drums and finger cymbals, its ecstatic dance, its lively scents, and its colorful sights. I had followed with consuming interest the many stories of Krishna's pranks and exploits that still echo through the crowded streets of that magical city. I had felt close to God throughout all of this, without for a moment sensing any distance from the Lord Jesus or from the God I know and love in Him. In my heart there was no question to be raised. As a Christian I was praising God and enjoying God's presence in ways I had never expected. Still, though my heart raised no questions, perhaps because I am a professor, maybe even an "intellectual," my head did. So I had to ask them, to myself and to anyone who would listen.

If the reader of this introduction expects to find any answer to these questions in my comments here, he or she will be sorely disappointed. Nonetheless, I warmly welcome a book which demonstrates that I am not the only one asking them. The best I can do, perhaps, is to remind the reader that such questions have been asked for a very long time and by many, many people, and that no definitive answer has yet been spoken. This book, therefore, does not close the conversation. It does not pretend its answers are final. Rather it takes up the conversation, continues it in an open-hearted and compelling way, makes its own distinctive contribution, and invites further thought and reflection.

This is as it should be. Both those who follow Jesus of Nazareth and those who serve Lord Krishna know full well that the Truth of God is larger, more complex, more multi-faceted, and vastly more intricate than either of our traditions can encompass. No one should claim to have said the last word about these questions. In fact if anyone does make such a claim, I would have serious doubts about that person's grasp of the divinity of love and mystery and compassion that constitute the reality of God.

In the earliest days of Christian history, theologians used to ask "What has Athens to do with Jerusalem?" They were asking what the ancient wisdom of the Greek philosophers had to do with the truth they believed had been revealed through God's covenant with the Jewish people and, through Jesus Christ, the Jewish rabbi who became the One who opened that covenant to the whole world. Although a minority of those early theologians, the most narrow-minded, argued that there was nothing to be learned from Athens, the verdict eventually went the other way. Wiser heads prevailed, and it was recognized that God had also been present in some mysterious way in Socrates and Plato, as well as in Jeremiah and St. Paul. Christ had not come to annul all previous truth, but to purify and transfigure it. Eventually Christian theologians came to see that if God is truth, then all truth must be of God. Thus the challenge the early church fathers took on was that of reconciling the truths of philosophy with those of revelation. That huge and ambitious task preoccupied Christian theology for nearly two millenia. St. Augustine drew on his philosophical and rhetorical training as a neo-Platonist in writing *The City of God*. St. Thomas Aquinas saw the challenge of reconciling Aristotle's philosophy and Christian

v

revelation as his life work. The result is that Christian theology remains, even today, an admixture of the Bible and categories of classical Western philosophy.

This historical legacy makes it both easier and more difficult for Christians to ask this question I am asking about Christ and Krishna. It is made easier by the fact that there is obviously a precedent for this kind of conciliatory thinking. If, upon reflection, Christians eventually decided that Jerusalem did have something to do with Athens, why can we not also say today that Nazareth has something to do with Vrindaban? But responding to the question is also made more difficult, ironically, by the same centuries-long Western Christian theological undertaking, because its result was that our thinking about the significance of Jesus is almost hopelessly enmeshed in a maze of "Western" intellectual and metaphysical categories. This means that before we can even *ask* about Christ and Krishna, let alone come to any satisfactory answer, we must disentangle the Man of Galilee, as He comes to us in the gospels of the New Testament, from the complex christologies and contending atonement theories which often seem to imprison the One we believe is the Lord of Life in desiccated theories and static dogmatic formulas.

Notice that my own personal question, like the title of this book, is not about "Christianity and Hinduism." These are both, after all, abstractions. "Christianity" usually refers to the system of beliefs and practices which emerged in the world in response to the life, death, and resurrection of Jesus. Although some of this is no doubt faithful and to His spirit, much of it—any thoughtful Christian must concede—is little more than excrescence and even distortion. As for "Hinduism," the term may be even more misleading. It indiscriminately lumps together all the many thousands of ways the people of the great sub-continent of India know and serve God. I do not believe a comparison of "Christianity" with "Hinduism" ever gets very far. Comparing vague abstractions and cultural generalizations never does. So I am asking a different question: what has Christ to do with Krishna?

Since the reader is no doubt eager to get on to what the author of this book says in response to this question I will not set forth any answers to it. But I will give a couple of hints.

First, let me say that as a Christian I am grateful that devotees of Krishna believe the One God reveals Himself (or Herself, for God is beyond gender) as a *person*, not as a concept or law or ritual. All these have their place in the life of faith, I am sure. But in a world-age that increasingly spurns the value of people, I find a welcome correlation between Christ and Krishna as *persons*. Many Westerners, when they first heard about "Hinduism," were told it was an impersonal kind of religion in which God was a kind of process, but had no face. Although this teaching about God is accurate in its description of some Indian religious philosophies, it most certainly does not describe the God who is known and served in Krishna.

Second, I am glad that in a world so filled with hatred, division, and contention, the God of Krishna is One of love, harmony, and reconciliation. Sometimes Christians are surprised that Krishna has a strong bond of love with a woman, whereas the Gospels give us only vague hints of Jesus' relationship with Mary Magdalene and other women in His entourage. Yet we know the Bible also uses nuptial imagery, in the Song of Songs for example, and in symbolizing the Church as Christ's bride. The inner meaning of both insights is that love partakes of the divine. Love is not optional but is central. As Christians put it, perhaps as strongly as it can be put: "God *is* Love."

No, I did not become a devotee in Vrindaban, or after my return. I remain a Christian and always will. Sometimes I visit a temple here in the U.S. When I do I feel free to clap and chant. I love to ponder the timeless message of the *Bhagavad-Gita*, and I am persuaded that people of every faith have something vital to learn from it. (Like the *Sermon on the Mount* it transcends religious boundaries.) But in the end

I return to the One I meet by the shores of the Jordan, the One who invites me to know God by following Him as He teaches and heals, feeds the hungry, sides with the poor and the disinherited, and faces down the oppressors with the courage of non-violent love. As a Christian I have been blessed and enriched by the Divine Spirit I felt in Vrindaban, and I am surer than I am of most things that that Spirit is the same One who came to dwell among us in a stable and died on a cross to conquer death.

You may, of course, ask me how I know. My answer will be unsatisfactory; I don't know how I know. But I do know. And, being the searcher that I am, I continue to ask. If the reader also asks these questions, also knows but doesn't know, also wants to go deeper into this old-but-ever-new question, then I invite him or her to proceed with this book. A rich feast awaits.

For several years now, devotees have asked me to write a book on Christianity and Krishna consciousness. It is, of course, easy to understand why this particular topic interests us so much. Practically all of us Westerners who have taken to Krishna consciousness were in some way previously involved in Judeo-Christian religion, and we naturally want to know how our current religious experience relates to that background and heritage.

Another need for the book has arisen within our community at New Vrindaban. Since the opening of Prabhupada's Palace of Gold, large numbers of pilgrims and guests have been coming daily. Because most are Christian, they also want to understand how our worship relates to theirs.

We are happy for this opportunity to explain the non-sectarian philosophy of Krishna consciousness, for Srila Prabhupada was very insistent on the point that there is only one religion: loving God with the whole heart. This is the essence of Christianity, and the practical application of Lord Krishna's demand that we abandon all varieties of religion and surrender unto Him only.

It is perhaps natural that the devotees looked to me to clarify these questions, for not only was I one of Prabhupada's first disciples, but my own background was steeped in the Christian tradition. Both my father and mother were Conservative Baptists of intense conviction, and I inherited their fervor. My earliest recollections are of spiritual experiences, and the religious life has never been far from my mind.

Over the years, it has been a great privilege for me to debate and discuss these topics with many Christian friends. Talks of transcendental subject matters are always relished by devotees of the Lord, no matter what their external commitment. Indeed, it is on the basis of such exchanges that we find the common ground of divine love, which provides the antidote to the godlessness and atheism now sweeping the world. It is imperative that we join together in this undertaking, otherwise we may all perish separately. Never have the forces of evil been so rampant or so aggressive, but on the other hand, never has the mercy of the Lord and the means for developing our dormant love of God been so easily available. Lord Krishna Chaitanya specifically descended to inundate the whole world with pure love of God, and the Hare Krishna movement seeks to fulfill His desire.

This book includes a number of discussions with Christian leaders, as well as a series of radio shows recorded in 1982 and 1983. Most of the radio questions were compiled by my good friend and Godbrother, Hayagriva das. The spontaneous answers have been expanded to further elucidate points raised by devotees and guests. It is my sincere wish to help bring about a new era of peace and brotherhood through a common understanding of our great religious faiths, and their relationship to the Supreme Father of all faiths. Hare Krishna!

Kirtanananda Swami Bhaktipada
July 22, 1985

Left: His Divine Grace A.C. Bhaktivedanta Swami Prabhupada, Founder-*Acharya* of the International Society for Krishna Consciousness.
Right: His Divine Grace Kirtanananda Swami Bhaktipada, Founder and Spiritual Master of the New Vrindaban Community.

Left: The Divine Guru C.C. gives a discourse on world problems at a regular Session at the International Society for Krishna Consciousness.

Right: The Divine Guru expounds on Vedic, Shakspeare, Sumer, and Spiritual Maxims at the New Vrindaban Community.

CHAPTER ONE

Christianity And Krishna Consciousness

Question: We understand that your father was a Baptist minister and that you were raised a Christian. Can you tell us a little about your background?

Srila Bhaktipada: I was a very devout child, and I used to gather my friends together and preach to them. My father was such a conservative minister that he even considered all other Christian denominations to be somewhat pagan. In any case, as a child, I used to try to convert my friends to the Baptist church.

Question: You were very much convinced at that time?

Srila Bhaktipada: Oh, yes.

Question: Why did you give up that faith?

Srila Bhaktipada: In our culture, when one becomes a teenager, it is fashionable to reject everything. Of course, this is very gradual. Being subjected to these cultural influences, I began to question my religion, and I was unable to get satisfactory answers. I wanted to know who I was, why I was here, and why I should believe in God. I began asking questions like "What is God?" "What is the relevance of God to modern man?" When I did not get satisfactory answers, I rejected my religion. Years later, when Srila Prabhupada came and presented satisfactory answers, I accepted Him as my spiritual master. It was because He answered my questions that I accepted Him. Of course, He happened to be a pure devotee of Lord Krishna.

Question: Then, when you came to Krishna consciousness, you asked the same questions?

1

Srila Bhaktipada: Yes. Srila Prabhupada answered my previously unanswered questions. This isn't to say that Christianity has no answers. I am not condemning any bona fide religion because the principles of bona fide religion are the same everywhere. Religion means the laws of God. One who abides by these laws is truly religious. The laws of God, as stated in all scriptures, demand surrender to God. This was taught by Lord Jesus Christ when the Pharisees asked Him, "Which is the great commandment in the law?" Christ answered: "Thou shalt love the Lord thy God with all thy heart, and with all thy soul, and with all thy might. This is the first and great commandment." (Matt 22.37-38) Love means surrender. In *Bhagavad-gita*, Lord Krishna imparted the same message of surrender in love and devotion.

Question: Has your understanding of Christ changed?

Srila Bhaktipada: Yes. Previously I was taught that one must choose Christ and condemn all others, but now I know that only those who deny God are condemned. In Krishna consciousness, we consider Jesus Christ to be the perfect son of God because He does the work of His Father perfectly. Since this is the case, it is not surprising to see a similarity between the New Testament of Jesus Christ and the *Bhagavad-gita* of Lord Krishna. Indeed, *Bhagavad-gita* is sometimes referred to as the New Testament of Hinduism.

Question: Is this to say that you don't find any basic difference between the essence of Christianity and Krishna consciousness?

Srila Bhaktipada: Not at all. Jesus Christ says to love God, and Krishna says, "Love Me." What is the difference? Jesus Christ says to love the Father, and Krishna says, "I am the Father of all living entities. Surrender unto Me." Where is the contradiction?

Question: How do you understand Christ's identity? Who is Christ?

Srila Bhaktipada: If we want to understand Christ, we should begin by understanding His name. In Krishna consciousness, as well as in the Judaeo-Christian tradition, there is unity between the name of God and God Himself. This is also true of God's representative, the spiritual master. God and His name are nondifferent. Similarly, the names given to Jesus are identical with Him. There are many references to this in the Bible: "At the name of Jesus every knee should bow, of things in heaven, and things in earth, and things under the earth. And that every tongue should confess that Jesus Christ is Lord, to the glory of God the Father." (Phil 2.10-11) Or, "For whosoever shall call upon the name of the Lord shall be saved." (Romans 10.13)

The name of Christ also reveals something about the character of Christ. There are many names mentioned in the New Testament, but His given name, Jesus, is derived from the Hebraic name Joshua, or Jahveh, meaning salvation, or deliverance. Jesus is so called because he saves or delivers His followers from sin. "And thou shalt call His name Jesus: for He shall save His people from their sins." (Matt 1.21) Christ's primary mission was to save people from sinful activity, and therefore from hell. Hell, after all, is simply a consequence of sin. As soon as we commit sin, we've already created our hell because we have separated ourselves from God. Due to disobedience, Adam hid himself from God. It is not that God has to personally punish us for our sins. We punish ourselves by separating ourselves from our beloved Father, who is all good and perfect. In this way, we create our own hellish condition.

Christ came to save people from their sins by showing them how to surrender to God and follow His will. Therefore followers of Christ call Him Lord because He is the ruler of their lives. And He is called the Messiah, or the anointed one, because He was especially appointed, or anointed, by God to save people from material existence. The Messiah is one who comes in the name of God to deliver God's message and save people from sinking into the most hellish condition. In the Book of Acts, Christ is also called servant, savior, and redeemer. What is He redeeming us from? From this miserable material condition in which we forget our eternal loving relationship with God. The spirit soul is eternally part and parcel of God, but due to forgetfulness, we identify with these material bodies. Therefore we think, "I am American, I am Russian, I am Indian, I am black, white, male, female, and so on." These are all bodily designations. To be redeemed means to transcend all these false designations and come back to our original spiritual consciousness in which we can understand ourselves in relationship with God.

Unfortunately, most people are going through life without even considering this. We all have an eternal relationship with God, and it was Christ's mission to redeem us from materialistic thinking and remind us of our eternal, spiritual identity. Christ even called Himself the son of man* to emphasize that man has a special relationship with God, for man is created in the image and likeness of God. We should not come into this world to lord it over material nature but to serve the Father as dutiful sons. Christ Himself always set the example of this in His obedience and humility, not only before God but also before man, and even before His enemies. The word "Christ," or "Christos," is the Greek translation of the Hebraic "Messiah," and also means "the anointed one." Again, the idea is that Christ was anointed by God to deliver mankind from bondage to sin. In the Vedas, one who has been thus anointed, or appointed, is called an *avatara*, or "one who descends" from the spiritual world to carry out God's mission. There are different kinds of avatars. We recognize Christ as a *shaktavesh-avatara*, a living entity especially empowered by God for a particular mission. Because He descends directly from the Kingdom of God, He is God's representative. Being uncontaminated, He is not of this world.

Question: Christ is called "God's only begotten son." But then, aren't we all sons of God? How is Christ different?

Srila Bhaktipada: It is a fact that God is the original Father of every living entity. We are all His sons. "For as many as are led by the spirit of God, they are the sons of God." (Romans

---

*Christ most frequently referred to Himself as the son of man: fourteen times in Mark, thirty times in Matthew, twenty-five times in Luke, and thirteen times in John.

8.14) In the beginning, there was only God, and from Him all creation proceeds. Logically, this means that we are all the offspring of God. When Jesus Christ calls Himself the son of God, or refers to God as "my Father," or "the Father," He is indirectly saying that we are also God's sons, for He has declared Himself to be the son of man.

What is the difference between us and Jesus Christ? Most significantly, Christ is never separated from God. "I and my Father are one." (John 10.30) But we, due to our sinful activity, have become separate in interest. With a rebellious attitude, we have come into this material world to try to enjoy material nature against God's benevolent desire. Jesus Christ never did this. In fact, His love of God was so great that He was willing to do God's work even though it meant crucifixion. Christ's love of God was unique in quality, but at the same time we should understand that, as sons of God, we all have that potential to love God perfectly. "Be ye therefore perfect, even as your Father which is in heaven is perfect." (Matt 5.48)

If we give up our selfish desires—or our very lives—in order to serve God, then we are following Christ. According to St. Paul: "I beseech you therefore, brethren...that ye present your bodies a living sacrifice, holy, acceptable unto God, which is your reasonable service." (Romans 12.1) It is not that we have to be literally crucified daily, but we should sacrifice our separate desires, the desire for personal sense gratification, in order to serve God unconditionally.

Question: What of Christ's teaching that no one can come to the Father except through Him?

Srila Bhaktipada: We say something similar when we say that one has to approach the Supreme Lord through the pure devotee, who is known as *jagad-guru*, the universal guru. It is the *jagad-guru* who speaks the Word. "In the beginning was the Word, and the Word was with God, and the Word was God."(John 1.1) Christ Himself claimed to be this very Word, and this Word is one. Christ says that no one can approach God directly; one must approach Him through the Word, the *jagad-guru.* We agree.

Often Christ is misunderstood when He claims to be the only son of God. This is not meant quantitively but qualitatively. When we reach perfection by rendering complete service to the Lord, the Lord reciprocates in a relationship so unique that it appears to the Lord's pure devotee that he alone in the entire universe is thus favored by God. This is the nature of spiritual loving exchanges. Each and every *gopi* who danced with Krishna thought that Krishna was dancing with her only. When Chaitanya Mahaprabhu danced before the Ratha-yatra cart, He appeared in each and every kirtan party, and each party thought that Lord Chaitanya was exclusively with them.

By His inconceivable energy, the Supreme Lord can expand Himself in the heart of each devotee in a unique way, so that it seems that each is the only son. Why should God have only one son? Even a mere human being can have dozens. God, being infinite, can have billions and trillions of sons, and by His inconceivable energy, each and every one can be His only son. That is the mystery of the relationship awakened with Krishna by pure devotional service.

Question: You've said that Krishna is God the Father. This would mean that Christ is Krishna's son. Wouldn't most Christians protest that this makes Krishna greater than Christ?

Srila Bhaktipada: We are answering only according to Christ's own words: "When ye have lifted up the Son of man, then shall ye know that I am he, and that I do nothing of myself; but as my Father hath taught me, I speak these things." (John 8.28) Or, "The son can do nothing of himself, but what he seeth the Father do." (John 5.19)

Because Jesus Christ always recognizes the supremacy of the Father, He is always in perfect harmony with the Father. "I go unto the Father, for my Father is greater than I." (John 14.28) He is the perfect servant of the Father. We are not proclaiming something new. Christ identifies Himself as the son of the Father, and, accepting Christ's word as truth, we must agree. Why should we try to make Him into something else?

His glory is in being the perfect son. We should simply try to follow His example, His teachings, and obey the commandments of the Father, as Christ Himself obeyed them. When we do so, we also become God's true sons, having the same interest as our Father.

Question: Although you're pointing out that there are no essential differences between Christianity and Krishna consciousness, obviously some differences exist, don't they?

Srila Bhaktipada: There may be differences in degree, but the final principle is the same. Both Christ and Krishna were teaching surrender to God. That is the essence. But Lord Chaitanya, for example, has taught us surrender up to the very point of conjugal love. This was never taught before. In Christianity, we are taught to love God in the father-son relationship. That is, God is worshipped as a father, and the perfected living entity is His son. The father's principal duty is to provide for his child, while the duty of the child is to beg from and obey the father. In Krishna consciousness, this is called the master-servant relationship, because God is viewed as the supreme master, or Father, and all living entities as His servants or sons.

It is certainly possible for a loving relationship to develop between master and servant, but the intensity and spontaneity of the loving relationship is limited by awe and reverence. It is not as intimate a love as we find between friends who consider themselves equal. When friends of similar standing want to serve one another without any strictures of formality or fear, the relationship becomes more intimate.

Higher than this is the love that parents feel for their child. Mother Yasoda and Nanda Maharaja displayed such love for Krishna as their dearmost son. Similarly, Mary and Joseph had such affection for the Christ child. When we worship God as Father, our tendency is to pray, "Give me, give me, give me." But if God becomes our son, we will think, "If I don't feed and care for Him properly, He may die." This is exactly how Mother Yasoda thought of Krishna.

This is certainly a very highly developed stage of love of God, but still higher than parental affection is the love found between lovers. Krishna became the lover of Radharani and of all the other *gopis*, and that most intimate, pure, conjugal relationship is explained in great detail only by Lord Chaitanya Mahaprabhu. If we want to learn to love God with the totality and surrender that only a true lover has for his beloved, then we have to take lessons from Sri Chaitanya Mahaprabhu.

Question: Many people say, "I love God very much," but how can we compare the love felt in these relationships? What is the test?

Srila Bhaktipada: Bhismadeva defined love as completely reposing our affections in one person. As long as affection is divided, it is not pure love. "No man can serve two masters, for either he will hate the one, and love the other; or else he will hold to the one, and despise the other. Ye cannot serve God and mammon." (Matt 6.24) But in a higher sense, love is actually not possible in the material world, because no one can surrender completely to another conditioned soul. Krishna is the only truly loveable object in the universe because He is altogether lovely. He is the fountainhead of all attractive qualities: beauty, strength, fame, wealth, knowledge, and renunciation. Only He can accept our whole love; therefore love of God is the only real love possible. So-called loving feelings in this material world are but perverted reflections of our innate love for God. When love is perverted, it is expressed as lust. Love for anything other than God is lust, though the deluded world may call it love.

Question: Then Christ did not tell His disciples anything essentially different from what's taught in the literatures of Krishna consciousness?

Srila Bhaktipada: As I said, it is not a difference in kind but in quantity. Christ Himself told His disciples, "I have yet many things to say unto you, but ye cannot bear them now." (John 16.12) In the Old Testament, God appears as a burning bush, a dove, a pillar of fire by night, a cloud by day, and so forth, but He does not appear in His original form, as He is. God the Father remains little known. Christ said, "Ye have neither heard His voice at any time, nor seen His shape....Not that any man hath seen the Father save he which is of God, he hath seen the Father." (John 5.37, 6.46). In the Bible, we find God described as great, angry, terrible, greatly to be feared, almighty, the everlasting Father, the alpha and omega, and so on, but God's all-attractive personality remains hidden.

What are God's features? His opulences? His activities? What does He Himself feel? What are His various manifestations? Specifically, how does He create? How does He pervade His creation? These and many other questions are neither raised nor answered in the Bible. Still, the essential truth is the same in Christianity and Krishna consciousness. The difference is in detail. Is an abridged dictionary different from an unabridged one? Yes and no. The basic definitions are there, but in the abridged dictionary only one or two definitions may be given, whereas in the unabridged dictionary dozens of definitions and nuances may be described. The Vedic literatures contain the most complete information about God. For instance, from Genesis we learn that "In the beginning God created the heaven and the earth," (Gen 1.1) and we receive a general description of the creation, but exactly how God created is not explained. In the Vedic literatures, the complete process of creation, maintenance, and annihilation is described.

Question: Is Christ mentioned?

Srila Bhaktipada: Not directly, but His characteristics are described. Six different kinds of incarnation are mentioned: *lila-avatara*, *manvantara-avatara*, *shaktavesh-avatara*, *guna-avatara*, *purusha-avatara*, and *yuga-avatara*. Jesus Christ is a *shaktavesh-avatara*, especially empowered to carry out a specific mission on behalf of God. That mission was to save the world from sin. This is the mission of all seers of the truth, and according to time and circumstances, that eternal truth, *sanatan dharma*, is promulgated.

Question: Christians accept Christ as coming directly from the Kingdom of God. Do you agree?

Srila Bhaktipada: Christ said, "I came forth from the Father, and am come into the world: again, I leave the world, and go to the Father." (John 16.28) Also: "I proceeded forth and came from God; neither came I of myself, but He sent me." (John 8.42) We cannot take our information from mental speculation. Spiritual things cannot be known that way. We have to know everything on the basis of spiritual authority. Jesus Christ was such an authority. "For He taught them as one having authority, and not as the scribes." (Matt 7.29) Such authority cannot be found in a mundane scholar. Therefore Christ came from Vaikuntha, the spiritual sky, or Kingdom of God, and when He left this planet, He returned there.

Question: Does this mean that Christ has His own abode in the spiritual sky?

Srila Bhaktipada: Yes. This is not uncommon. Great representatives of God, or God's expansions, have their own spiritual planets in the spiritual world, where they reside and teach Krishna consciousness. Just as Krishna has His own abode, Goloka Vrindaban, where He personally resides with His devotees, there are countless expansions of God in the spiritual sky with their own planets. "In my Father's house there are many mansions." (John 14.4) The Kingdom of God is full in all variety, and we can serve the Lord there according to our specific propensity.

Question: What was Christ's specific mission in coming here from the spiritual world?

Srila Bhaktipada: To preach love of God. When asked what is the great commandment, Christ said, "Thou shalt love the Lord thy God with all thy heart, and with all thy soul, and with all thy mind." (Matt. 22.37) And then, the obvious corollary: "Thou shalt love thy neighbor as thyself." (Matt. 22.39) Once we love God and see that everything is connected to Him, we can understand that all living beings are part and parcel of God. Then we cannot mistreat even an ant.

Question: If love of God is the common goal in both Christianity and Krishna consciousness, why are the means so different?

Srila Bhaktipada: The ceremonies may be different due to differences in culture and circumstance, but the basic philosophy is the same. Loving God means giving up this material conception of life. Whether we follow Christianity, Krishna consciousness, Mohammedanism, or Buddhism, we have to become detached from worldly pleasures. That is, we have to abandon the misconception that we can be happy in this world. "My kingdom is not of this world." (John 18.36) Throughout the Bible, we are warned against "the world, the flesh, and the devil," and in *Bhagavad-gita* we are warned against coming under the sway of the senses. "An intelligent person does not take part in the sources of misery, which are due to contact with the material senses. Such pleasures have a beginning and an end, and so the wise man does not delight in them." (Bg. 5.22) The message is the same: we cannot be happy in this world by material sense gratification.

Nor is it possible to be spiritual and materialistic at the same time. "Ye cannot serve God and mammon." (Matt. 6.24) Moreover, "If any man will come after me, let him deny himself, and take up his cross, and follow me." (Matt 16.24) Death to self and then a new life in God is the essence of *bhakti-yoga*, or Krishna consciousness. To become the Lord's pure devotee, we have to be willing to sacrifice everything of this world for His satisfaction. "All that you do, all that you eat, all that you offer and give away, as well as all austerities that you may perform, should be done as an offering unto Me." (Bg. 9.27)

God's message is the same in all religions: "Surrender unto Me. Give up your vain attempts to be lord of this world, for your nature is subordinate to Mine. You are eternally My servant." Of course, the externals may appear different because God's representative speaks for the understanding of a particular people. Many of Christ's disciples were common, uneducated fishermen. Some were even illiterate. He was not speaking to enlightened souls who were already cultured in spiritual knowledge. He had to speak differently from Lord Chaitanya, who spoke to the highly elevated Ramananda Roy, or Lord Krishna, who spoke to the valiant warrior Arjuna on the battlefield of Kurukshetra. But the message was essentially the same: Give up attachment to the bodily conception, surrender to God, and fight the good fight.

Question: Christ is often called the redeemer because He saved mankind through His death on the cross. Similarly, Krishna is called Mukunda, the granter of liberation, because He frees man from bondage to material life. Can you explain the significance of Christ the redeemer and Krishna the liberator?

Srila Bhaktipada: Yes, Christ redeems His follower by enabling him to stop breaking the laws of God. And Krishna liberates His devotee by enlightening him as to his innate spiritual nature, thereby removing the bodily conception of life that forces one to commit sin. If we don't stop sinning, there is no question of being either redeemed or liberated. "Not everyone that saith unto me, Lord, Lord, shall enter into the kingdom of heaven; but he that doeth the will of my Father which is in heaven." (Matt 7.21) Stopping further sinful activity is absolutely necessary for a true disciple of Krishna, Christ, or guru, or any bona fide representative of God.

Question: Christ is said to redeem mankind because He is the perfect sacrifice, "the Lamb of God which taketh away the sins of the world." (John 1.29) But why would a benevolent God send His own special son to suffer so? Why must God be appeased by blood sacrifice?

Srila Bhaktipada: It is not that God is appeased by the blood of animal or human sacrifice. God does not have to be appeased. According to the Old Testament, "to obey is better than sacrifice." (I Samuel 15.22)) If we obey the laws of God, there is no need for sacrifice. What is required is knowledge of God's laws and obedience to them. "For I desired mercy, and not sacrifice; and the knowledge of God more than burnt offerings." (Hosea 6.6) Christ came to convince man of God's laws, but because men were so degraded, He had to die on the cross to convince them of the consequences of sin. But why keep Christ on the cross? St. Paul says that those who commit sinful activity "crucify to themselves the Son of God afresh." (Heb 6.6) If we say that Christ died for our sins and yet continue sinning, we are crucifying Christ over and over. If we actually love Christ, or Krishna, or guru, we have to give up sinning. "If ye love me, keep my commandments." (John 14.15) By obeying the laws of God, we show that we love God.

Question: When Krishna lived on this earth, did He demand sacrifice?

Srila Bhaktipada: Certainly. "Whatever a man may sacrifice to other gods is really meant for Me alone, but it is offered without true understanding. I am the only enjoyer and the only object of sacrifice." (Bg. 9.23-24) And of all sacrifices, the best is *japa*, the chanting of the holy names of God. "Of sacrifices," Krishna says, "I am the chanting of the holy names." (Bg. 10.25)

God is not different from His name. When we, His fallen sons, call out in love and affection by chanting His names, we are offering the best sacrifice. For our own good, the Lord wants us to obey His laws. He wants our surrender, which is the symptom of our love. He doesn't want us to kill innocent animals, or slaughter our children. He is all loving and all merciful, and He is especially affectionate to those who call on His name. A parent naturally attends to his child when he hears him call out, "Father! Father!" Similarly, the Lord is pleased when we turn our attention toward Him and sincerely cry out, "Hare Krishna! Hare Krishna! My dear Lord! Please pick me up from this ocean of birth and death and again engage me in Your transcendental loving service. Make me again Your eternal servant, and take me back home, back to Godhead."

Question: What is the importance of Christ's death on the cross and subsequent resurrection?

Srila Bhaktipada: When Christ died on the cross, He made the ultimate sacrifice. His passion and crucifixion were the greatest expression of love for God. By showing us how to love God, He became the standard by which we can approach God. His resurrection is, therefore, "the firstfruits of the spirit." (Romans 8.23) He showed us that beyond this material body is a spiritual body not subject to corruption, nor polluted by muscle, veins and blood. That spiritual body is *sat-chit-ananda*—eternal, full of knowledge and bliss. In that spiritual body, we can engage in wonderful spiritual pastimes with the Lord in the Kingdom of God, world without end.

CHAPTER TWO

The Meaning Of God

Question: By way of definition, could you first explain the origin and meaning of the English word "God"?

Srila Bhaktipada: The word "God" has a very ancient and interesting history. Surprisingly, it can be traced back to Sanskrit through the Old Teutonic language: *gudo*, *ghudho*, *gheu*, and *hu*. The Sanskrit meaning is "to invoke, to pour, to offer sacrifice." In Sanskrit, *puru-huta* means "much invoked," and is a name of Indra, who is worshipped by sacrifice. So the word "God" in English originally meant "that which is invoked," or, "the object of worship." The idea is that God is the supreme power in the universe, and His worship is necessary for welfare and happiness. Worship of God is innate in all men and can be found in all cultures. That the etymology points back to Sanskrit is just another proof that Vedic culture is the original culture.

Of course, there are different conceptions of God, but they all have one thing in common: God is superior power. Beyond our immediate perception, there is a controller—God—or many controllers, gods. Lower living entities see higher living entities as gods, or controllers. For an insect, an animal is a god. For an animal, a man is a god, and for a man, higher beings are gods. In the universal government, there are many controllers: Indra controls the rain, Vayu controls the wind, Agni controls fire, Varuna controls the seas, and so forth. These controllers are called demigods, or *devas* in Sanskrit. Now, He whom no one controls and who controls all others and everything that be is called God, the supreme controller.

15

That is God with a capital G. There are many gods, but only one God. He is Absolute: omniscient, omnipresent, and omnipotent. He is immanent in His creation as the impersonal Brahman effulgence, the Supreme Spirit, and simultaneously is transcendent as the Supreme Person.

Generally, when people hear the word "God," they think of the creator, but God is more than the creator. He is also the maintainer and destroyer. In Christianity, there is sometimes confusion over God's role: Does He simply create and then let nature take its course? Do demonic forces destroy? But according to the Vedic conception, God acts in three stages: creation, maintenance, and destruction. As Brahma, He creates; as Vishnu, He preserves; and as Shiva, He destroys. Creation and preservation have the common characteristic that all beings continuously owe their existence to His power. He is the sustainer as well as the first cause, and in the end, all things are merged to rest in Him. "Of all creations, I am the beginning, and the end, and also the middle," Krishna says. (Bg. 10.32) Going beyond this, in *Srimad-Bhagavatam*, He declares: "Brahma, it is I, the Personality of Godhead, who was existing before the creation, when there was nothing but Myself. Nor was there the material nature, the cause of this creation. That which you see now is also I, the Personality of Godhead, and after annihilation what remains will also be I, the Personality of Godhead." (Bhag. 2.9.33) In the final analysis, everything that exists is part of God, and it is all emanating from His Supreme Personality.

Question: Has the word "God" always referred to a supreme being?

Srila Bhaktipada: No, the word can refer to any controller. Materialists usually worship a demigod, someone who is very powerful but not supreme, because they are interested in aquiring some material benediction. For instance, the Greeks and Romans worshipped extraordinary persons such as Zeus, Apollo, or Mars, who had some power over nature and the fortunes of mankind. And today, such personalities continue to be worshipped, though under different names. These powers of inferior rank—heroes, idols, and demigods—can give some temporary boons, but they are not worshipped by intelligent men.

Although the Greeks worshipped many gods, the intelligent distinguished between demigods and the Supreme God. Common men are generally attached to inferior gods in order to get a good wife, education, or wealth, but intelligent men like Socrates are not. In fact, Socrates was condemned to death for discouraging such worship.

In the West, the belief in one Supreme God is found in the Old Testament: "Yahweh is One." This is also the Muslim belief: "There is no god but Allah." Christ, of course, proclaimed the unity of the Father, but Christians differ from the Jews and Muslims in their belief in the Trinity. Still, the Father, Son, and Holy Spirit are three aspects of a unified Godhead. A follower of the Vedas can understand this mystery of "three in One" because we also speak of three aspects of God: the impersonal Brahman, the localized Paramatma, and Bhagavan, the Supreme Personality of Godhead. Still, there is unity. Lord Krishna says, "By Me, in My unmanifested form, this entire universe is pervaded. All beings are in Me, but I am not in them....Although I am the maintainer of all living entities, and although I am everywhere, still My Self is the very source of creation." (Bg. 9.4-5)

Question: Aren't many gods still acknowledged in Hinduism? How do they differ from the Supreme God?

Srila Bhaktipada: The Supreme God is the origin and controller of all other gods. "Neither the hosts of demigods nor the great sages know My origin," Krishna says, "for in every respect, I am the source of the demigods and the sages." (Bg. 10.2) The Bible speaks of God as the Lord of lords, the King of kings. On earth, there may be many kings, but there is no one king ruling them all. Therefore there is competition and war. Only when the King of kings is ruling can there be peace. Only God, or His bona fide representative like Jesus Christ, can qualify as the King of kings. Until we revive our spiritual consciousness and recognize the authority of the Supreme Lord, peace on earth will remain a Utopian dream.

Of course, in India today we find many demigods worshipped: Kali, or Durga, is worshipped as the mistress of material nature. Ganesh is worshipped for success in commerce, and Saraswati is worshipped for knowledge or academic success. Shiva is also worshipped for a variety of material benedictions. But worship of the demigods is discouraged by Lord Krishna in *Bhagavad-gita:* "Those whose minds are distorted by material desires surrender unto demigods and follow the particular rules and regulations of worship according to their own natures. I am in everyone's heart as the Supersoul. As soon as one desires to worship the demigods, I make his faith steady so that he can devote himself to some particular deity. Endowed with such a faith, he seeks favors of a particular demigod and obtains his desires. But in actuality these benefits are bestowed by Me alone. Men of small intelligence worship the demigods, and their fruits are limited and temporary. Those who worship the demigods go to the planets of the demigods, but My devotees ultimately reach My supreme planet." (Bg. 7.20-23)

Worship of the demigods will not help us solve the problems of material existence: birth, old age, disease, and death. These problems can be solved only by worship of the Supreme Lord Himself. Only He is Mukunda, the liberator from the cycle of birth and death. Only He can redeem us. Therefore Lord Krishna says, "After many births and deaths, he who is actually in knowledge surrenders unto Me, knowing Me to be the cause of all causes and all that is. Such a great soul is very rare." (Bg. 7.19)

Question: You emphasize God's personality as Krishna, but in Hinduism the impersonalists, or Vedantists, deny Krishna's supremacy. They say that the formless Brahman is supreme. For them, it's not the person Krishna whom we're to worship, but the impersonal Absolute speaking through Krishna. Why is there this disagreement? And why do you emphasize worship of the person Krishna?

Srila Bhaktipada: It is very important to understand this point. The cause of everything is a person. We have no experience of anything coming from something impersonal. Behind energy, there is an energetic source, and in the Vedic scriptures this is confirmed to be the Supreme Person: *Brahmeti paramatmeti bhagavan iti sabdyate.* "Learned transcendentalists who know the Absolute Truth call this nondual substance Brahman, Paramatma, and Bhagavan." (*Srimad-Bhagavatam* 1.2.11) Brahman is the all-pervading impersonal aspect of God. Paramatma is the localized aspect, the Supersoul within the heart of every living being. And Bhagavan is the Supreme Personality of Godhead who resides eternally in His own abode, the Kingdom of God.

Complete understanding means realizing God in all three aspects. The impersonalists, or Vedantists, realize only the impersonal Brahman, and because they cling to this as the all-in-all, they cannot realize the other two aspects. When one understands the Paramatma, or Supersoul, he can also understand Brahman; that is, he understands two aspects, so his realization is higher than the impersonalist's. And when one realizes Bhagavan, the Supreme Person Himself, then he realizes all three aspects.

Impersonal Brahman realization may be compared to realization of the sunshine, which is all-pervading. Just as sunshine pervades this world, God pervades His creation. He is omnipresent. Paramatma realization is compared to realizing the sun disc itself. This means understanding the localized aspect: God in the heart. And Bhagavan realization is compared to realizing the sun god who lives within the sun disc and is himself the source of the disc, heat, and light. Bhagavan, the Supreme Personality of Godhead, is the source of the localized and all-pervasive aspects. *Brahmano hi pratisthaham.* Krishna says, "I am the basis of the impersonal Brahman." (Bg. 14.27) And: "I am in everyone's heart as the

Supersoul." (Bg. 7.21) "The yogi who knows that I and the
Supersoul within all creatures are one worships Me and remains always in Me in all circumstances." (Bg. 6.31) It is
the Supreme Person, Krishna, who is the source of all manifestations of Godhead.

We stress worship of the person Krishna because it is the
highest realization. We are not manufacturing something new.
This is not our own opinion, but the verdict of scripture. The
very opening of *Bhagavatam* declares: "O my Lord, Sri
Krishna, son of Vasudeva, O all-pervading Personality of
Godhead, I offer my respectful obeisances unto You. I meditate upon Lord Sri Krishna because He is the Absolute Truth
and the primeval cause of all causes of the creation, suste-
nance and destruction of the manifested universes. He is directly and indirectly conscious of all manifestations, and He
is independent because there is no other cause beyond Him.
It is He only who first imparted the Vedic knowledge unto
the heart of Brahmaji, the original living being. By Him even
the great sages and demigods are placed into illusion, as one
is bewildered by the illusory representations of water seen in
fire, or land seen on water. Only because of Him do the material universes, temporarily manifested by the reactions of
the three modes of nature, appear factual, although they are
unreal. I therefore meditate upon Him, Lord Sri Krishna, who
is eternally existent in the transcendental abode, which is
forever free from the illusory representations of the material
world. I meditate upon Him, for He is the Absolute Truth."
(Bhag. 1.1.1)

Eventually we must come to the point of realizing God as
a person. So why not now? "He whose mind is fixed on My
personal form, always engaged in worshipping Me with great
and transcendental faith, is considered by Me to be most perfect." (Bg. 12.2) Surrender to the Supreme Person is the perfection of all forms of yoga.

Question: Is Christianity basically personal or impersonal?
Srila Bhaktipada: Conservative, traditional Christianity also

stresses the personal feature. For the true Christian, God is the all-loving Supreme Person. He is the Supreme Father, the Friend, the Master, the King, the Christ. For the Christian, as well as the Krishna devotee, the personality of God can be known only through revelation. "No man hath seen God at any time; the only begotten Son, which is in the bosom of the Father, he hath declared Him." (John 1.18) No amount of speculation or austerity can enable us to know Him as He is. How can the infinite be known through finite, imperfect senses? We must await revelation. "For now we see through a glass, darkly; but then face to face: now I know in part; but then shall I know even as also I am known." (1 Cor 13.12)

Once we begin to render Him loving service, we reestablish our relationship with Him. This "I-Thou" relationship can only be with a Person. Of course, when we say "person" in reference to God, we mean a transcendent Person. He is not a finite person like us. His Personality is described in detail in the Vedic literatures, and by reading them we can come to understand what He looks like, how He acts, what His pastimes and activities are, why He descends into the world, in what ways His transcendental body differs from ours, and so on. This information cannot be attained by mental speculation. It must be received from scripture. It is said that if we want to know something of our father, we must consult our mother. Similarly, to know something of our Supreme Father, we must consult Mother Vedas.

Because the Bible gives very little information about God's personality, impersonalism has infiltrated Christianity in many ways, in all sects. We find it in Aquinas and Augustine, in Meister Eckhardt and Jacob Boehme, in Thomas Merton and Paul Tillich, in Baptist missions and in the Vatican. Impersonalism takes many forms, some subtle and some not. Sometimes priests speak of Christ not as a person but as "a spirit within us all." Some even go so far as to deny the historical Christ. This is all misleading. Srila Prabhupada has said that such impersonalism is worse than atheism. Impersonalists call themselves theists, but they try to kill God's personality. Therefore they are more dangerous than the atheists who come right out and say that God doesn't exist.

Confusion arises because people cannot understand the perfect philosophy of *acintya-bheda-bheda-tattva*: that is, God is simultaneously, inconceivably one with and different from His creation. He pervades every corner of His creation impersonally, but He still exists beyond the creation as the Supreme Person. Impersonalists are fond of saying, "Yes, God is everything. I am God. You are God. We are all God. God is everywhere. God is the Supreme Spirit. Christ is the spirit in everyone, etc." This may be all well and good, but the impersonalists stop there. When asked, "But doesn't God the Father reside in His heaven, the Kingdom of God?" the impersonalists reply, "Oh, you don't understand. That's an old-fashioned conception." In this way, they try to annihilate God's transcendental personality.

Lord Krishna explains the philosophy of simultaneous oneness and difference in this way: "By Me, in My unmanifested form, this entire universe is pervaded. All beings are in Me, but I am not in them. And yet everything that is created does not rest in Me. Behold My mystic opulence! Although I am the maintainer of all living entities, and although I am everywhere, still My Self is the very source of creation." (Bg. 9. 4-5)

To understand this philosophy, faith is needed. In this spirit, Christ taught us to pray, "Our Father, which art in heaven." Impersonalists, envious of the Almighty Father, try to take Him out of His heaven. They want paradise without God. Therefore the world has become atheistic. God has form, but His form is not material. God can be seen, but not with material eyes. We have to purify our vision. Therefore *Brahma-samhita* says: "I worship the primeval Lord, Govinda, who is always seen by the devotee whose eyes are anointed with the pulp of love. He is seen in His eternal form of Syamasundara situated within the heart of the devotee." (Bs 5.38)

Question: God has been called the all-perfect. Can you elaborate on this?

Srila Bhaktipada: Generally, by "perfect," we mean "whole," "entire," "intact." Perfection implies soundness, or excellence in every part, and "whole" suggests a completeness or perfection that cannot be sought, gained, or lost. "Entire" implies perfection derived from integrity. Being infinite, God possesses everything unlimitedly, including all qualities. He is all existence; therefore He is lacking nothing. Being eternal, he possesses everything simultaneously, forever. In praise of His eternal perfection, we could speak unlimitedly, but here we can only indicate what our finite minds can grasp.

The beautiful invocation of *Isopanishad* describes the perfection of God: "The Personality of Godhead is perfect and complete, and because He is completely perfect, all emanations from Him, such as this phenomenal world, are perfectly equipped as complete wholes. Whatever is produced of the complete whole is also complete in itself. Because He is the complete whole, even though so many complete units emanate from Him, He remains the complete balance." (*Isopanishad* Invocation)

If God were not complete, He could not be perfect. Being part and parcel of God, we are also perfect in connection with Him. As long as the part is connected to the whole, it acts perfectly, but if it is separated, it cannot. A severed hand may still look like a hand, but it is useless. Similarly, when we are connected to God, we are also perfect and complete, but when we are forgetful of Him, we become useless, and make a hell out of heaven.

Although we are all originally part and parcel of God, we are trying to live our lives separate from God in this material world, and therefore we are experiencing all kinds of imperfection. For instance, the material miseries of birth, old age, disease, and death are imperfections arising from forgetting our intimate relationship with God. Instead of seeing ourselves as spirit souls, eternal servants of God, we are seeing ourselves as these material bodies. This is called maya, illusion. And because of this, we are suffering. If we want to realize perfection, we have to surrender to God and return to Him.

Question: How did you personally come to understand that Krishna is the Supreme Personality of Godhead?

Srila Bhaktipada: We come to know God by meeting a friend of God. I am very fortunate to have met Srila Prabhupada, a pure devotee of Krishna. He taught me about God. Similarly, if you yourself want to know God, you also have to approach a bona fide representative of God, someone who actually knows God, who talks with God, works for God, and is always absorbed in thoughts of God. Such a pure devotee will instruct you in the nature of God. Realizing God is not very difficult. Although God cannot be seen with material eyes, He can be known very easily by His mercy and the mercy of His pure devotee. God has especially made Himself easily available by His name. Therefore the devotees are always chanting the holy names of Krishna. This is recommended in all scriptures: "Call upon the name of the Lord and thou shalt be saved." If we sincerely chant the holy names—Hare Krishna, Hare Krishna, Krishna Krishna, Hare Hare, Hare Rama, Hare Rama, Rama Rama , Hare Hare--we will come to understand the real meaning of God. We will realize Him as He is.

CHAPTER THREE

Proofs Of God's Existence

Question: Can God's existence be proved by our reasoning power alone? Apart from scriptural revelation, which is more or less a matter of faith, is there some rational, philosophical proof?

Srila Bhaktipada: By reason, we can certainly establish the necessity for God and the logical conclusion that He exists. *Achintya-bheda-bheda-tattva.* Although transcendental to His creation, God is also not different from it. The creation reflects God at every point. St. Paul writes, "For the invisible things of Him from the creation of the world are clearly seen, being understood by the things that are made, even His eternal power and Godhead; so that they [the ungodly] are without excuse." (Romans 1.20) Since visible things reflect the invisible, the atheistic mentality is illogical. God can be clearly seen in His creation, just as an inventor can be known by his invention. The invention doesn't simply happen by itself. Because the invention shows a logical design, it presupposes a designer, or creator. God is the author of this creation, and because He has personality, form, and senses, we too can have these qualities. Because He is rational, we can have reason. Indeed, He has made us rational creatures so that we can use our reason to know and understand Him.

Unfortunately, people today are misusing their rationality in an irrational pursuit of sense gratification. People are wasting their valuable human lives, their rational abilities, to exploit natural resources to meet the gross bodily demands: eating, sleeping, defending, and mating, which animals can do without the power of reason. As a result, people are forgetting God, becoming more and more illusioned, and losing their God-given reason and intelligence. And now we are beginning to see the logical consequences of all this: a suicidal nuclear arms race, social and moral disintegration, and increased suffering in the world.

Question: How is it that the unseen is proved by the seen? Can you give an example?

Srila Bhaktipada: The classic example: a clock presupposes a clockmaker. How can you have a perfect mechanism without a mechanic? The universe is a perfect mechanism with a perfect creator behind it. "This material nature is working under My direction," Krishna says, "and is producing all moving and unmoving beings." (Bg 9.10) Obviously the universe is the work of an intelligent being; otherwise, how can it work so precisely? Every year we see that the seasons are coming in perfect order: spring, summer, autumn, winter. They are not randomly mixed. The stars and planets throughout the universe are traveling in their course according to universal laws. We can see millions and billions of heavenly bodies functioning precisely in accordance with the laws of material nature. And God says, "These are My laws, working under My direction." Therefore the Psalmist says, "The fool hath said in his heart, There is no God." (Psalms 14.1)

Sooner or later, an intelligent person asks, "How are these great planets floating in space? How are the laws of nature working? Where does everything come from? What great intelligence has been able to imagine them, realize them, and put them in motion?" This universe is created, supported, and governed by an intelligent being whom we call God. "The heavens declare the glory of God, and the firmament showeth His handiwork." (Psalms 19.1) A person who cannot see God in the creation has lost his spiritual vision and become a blind fool.

Question: Some people argue that the world isn't perfect because there is evil and suffering. Is this so?

Srila Bhaktipada: No. That is due to their imperfect perspective. Actually the world is perfect, having been created by the all-perfect Personality of Godhead. Because He has given us independence, however, we can misuse His perfect gifts. If we were machines or robots, we would not have that independence. But out of His perfect knowledge, God has given us a certain measure of independence so that we can either voluntarily love Him and surrender to Him, or rebel against His authority and falsely claim that we are God. Without this freedom, there is no question of being able to love. Of what value is a robot's love? Freedom, or independence, is the foundation for the loving relationship between the living entity and the Lord; therefore there is always the chance that this independence can be misused, and that misuse is the cause of suffering.

It is not that God wants us to suffer, or that His creation is imperfect. Imperfection is due to our misuse of His perfection, and that is also perfect. We make such judgements due to our limited perspective. We have to understand the purpose behind nature's laws. For instance, if we put our hand into a fire, the hand is burned. That burning sensation is not wrong or bad. It is part of the body's defense mechanism, and is meant for our protection; otherwise we might leave the hand in the fire until it is consumed. From the overall viewpoint, it is for our total benefit.

Similarly, the suffering experienced in this material world—birth, old age, disease, and death—has a purpose. It is God's warning to us that we are not meant to be here. Something is out of joint. Material misery is a defense mechanism for the soul, telling him to get out of this material world. We are meant to live in the spiritual world, the kingdom of God, where existence is eternal, and full of knowledge and bliss. Through material nature, God has provided a self-protective system whereby the soul always feels anxious or uncomfortable while in this material world, but at the same time, the soul can never be harmed. "The soul can never be cut into pieces by any weapon, nor can he be burned by fire, nor moistened by water, nor withered by the wind. This individual soul is unbreakable and insoluble, and can be neither burned nor dried. He is everlasting, all-pervading, unchangeable, immovable, and eternally the same." (Bg. 2.23-24) Thus, material suffering is meant to drive us back home, back to the Kingdom of God. It is a great mistake to conclude that because suffering exists, the universe is imperfect, and therefore there is no God. Such a conclusion will only prolong our sojourn in this material world, and, therefore, our suffering.

Question: How do you answer scientists who claim that the universe just came about by chance?

Srila Bhaktipada: Can they give one example of a machine having come about by chance? Look at all the mechanisms we use in our daily lives: clocks and televisions, cars and computers, radios and cameras. Does anyone suggest that these things just happen, that there is no inventor, no company behind them? Behind any organized thing, there is an organizer. In a beautiful garden, we see the flowers arranged according to pattern. Is this by chance? Without a gardener, how long will the garden remain neat and trim? Behind every design, there is a designer.

The creation is very complex in all of its aspects, and whether we analyze a tiny atom or this immense universe, we can see organization exhibited in the laws of nature. How can an intelligent man say that there is no designer, no organizer? Just putting a small satellite into space requires many millions of dollars and thousands of scientists. But God is floating millions and billions of planets in space through His various energies. Are we to conclude that there is no energetic source behind the energy? No organizer behind the organization? No designer behind the design? How irrational to propose that all this has come about by chance! What they call "chance," we call "God."

Question: Traditionally, the argument of God as prime mover is cited as proof of God's existence. Can you explain this?

Srila Bhaktipada: We can see that matter is by nature inert. It cannot move by itself but requires some living, spiritual force. A car cannot move without the touch of a driver. We can see that there is motion in the universe; all these planets are moving, although in fact they are just huge rocks, or some other form of matter. We see the effects of motion, but what is its cause? What is that original force that sets the universe moving? What gave material nature its first push?

In Sanskrit, the word for that spiritual force is Purusha. God is called the Purusha, the energetic source, who activates inert Prakriti, material nature, and causes it to move. God is the one who pushes everything, the original cause of all movement. Therefore He is called the prime mover. In the form of Supersoul, or Paramatma, God enters into each and every atom and sets it in motion.

Question: According to the Big Bang theory, in the beginning there was a great lump of cosmic matter, or gases, and a great explosion followed, setting the universe in motion. Is this a possibility?

Srila Bhaktipada: Our first question is, "Where did that lump of original matter come from?" This, of course, scientists cannot answer. But, after all, that is the most important question. In World War II, there were many big bangs, but nothing positive came out of them. They were all destructive. The atomic explosions over Hiroshima and Nagasaki didn't create a television, radio, or computer. Then why should we think that some big bang created this precisely designed and marvelously varied universe?

The fact that so-called intelligent men can advance such theories is actually another proof of God's existence. "From Me come knowledge, remembrance, and forgetfulness," Krishna says (Bg 15.15) According to our desires, God helps us. Because these scientists want to deny God's existence, God helps them. Otherwise such absurd theories would be impossible for any sane man to contemplate. God is everywhere. His power is so great and His presence so compelling that we could not avoid God were it not for God's help. When we want to forget God, He helps us. If we so wish, we can forget Him forever. Mercifully, however, as soon as we want to know God and surrender to Him, He is there to help.

Question: What is meant by God as first cause, or the uncaused cause?

Srila Bhaktipada: That is the Vedic version:

> *isvarah paramah krsnah*
> *sac-cid-ananda-vigrahah*
> *anadir adir govindah*
> *sarva-karana-karanam*

"Krishna, who is known as Govinda, is the Supreme Godhead. He has an eternal, blissful, spiritual body. He is the origin of all. He has no other origin, and He is the prime cause of all causes." (*Brahma-samhita*)

In this material world, everything has its cause and effect. This is a world of duality, of relativity. But in the spiritual realm, where everything is absolute, cause and effect are one, eternally. God is all that exists before the creation, during the creation, and after annihilation. He is both cause and effect, and all that is. In the material world, a son has his father as cause, but that father in his turn was the effect of some other father, who also had a father, and on and on. If we try to trace out the original father, who had no father before him, we must come to God.

In the spiritual world, or in spiritual consciousness, all living beings are the sons of God, and that relationship is eternal. Actually all beings are sons of God in the past, present, and future, and God Himself is the original Father of everyone. "I am the seed-giving father of all living entities," Krishna says (Bg. 14.4). God is the original cause of all causes. All bona fide religions agree on this point.

Question: There is also the argument that because I have the idea of perfection, perfection must necessarily exist. Is this valid?

Srila Bhaktipada: Yes, living entities possess to some degree knowledge, beauty, wealth, fame, power, goodness, and so on, because these qualities exist originally and perfectly in God. If they were not in God, they could not exist in us. A son inherits the qualities of his father. He has two arms, two legs, and two eyes because his father has them. If we can think of perfection, which is beyond our experience, where does that thought come from? It must come from some higher perfection. Similarly, how could we begin to conceive of God, who is inconceivable, if God did not in fact exist with the inconceivable potency of revealing Himself to insignificant man?

Question: These formal, philosophical proofs of God's existence may be intellectually stimulating, but they can hardly satisfy the soul. What is the best method for understanding God's existence?

Srila Bhaktipada: *Sravanam kirtanam.* Hearing from authoritative sources, from the scriptures, and chanting. If we want to know the identity of our father, we had best consult our mother. God is our Father, and the scriptures are our mother. Without our mother's word, we can only guess who our father is. In Sanskrit, the scriptures are called *sruti,* "that which is heard." We have to hear about God from the scriptures, be they the Vedas, Bible, or Koran. Because these bona fide scriptures are directly spoken by God, or about God, they can satisfy the soul. We can hear from God through the scriptures and through the pure devotees following in disciplic succession from God. Such pure devotees never cheat or concoct new theories. They never contradict scripture, nor say, "I am God." Rather, they always point us toward that Supreme Person who is the cause of all causes. We can also personally experience God by chanting His holy names, which are nondifferent from Him. This process is called *kirtanam,* or kirtan. By chanting Hare Krishna, Hare Krishna, Krishna Krishna, Hare Hare, Hare Rama, Hare Rama, Rama Rama,

Hare Hare, we directly experience God by transcendental sound. God and His name are both absolute. Therefore the Psalmist writes: "O Lord, how excellent is Thy name in all the earth....I will praise Thy name for ever and ever.... Let them praise the name of the Lord: for His name alone is excellent.... Praise Him upon the loud cymbals: praise Him upon the high sounding cymbals. Let every thing that hath breath praise the Lord." (Psalms 8, 145, 148, 150) Hare Krishna!

CHAPTER FOUR

The Descent Of God

Question: How would you define an incarnation, or an avatar?

Srila Bhaktipada: First we can say what God is not. God is not a human being. Krishna says, "Fools deride Me when I descend in the human form. They do not know My transcendental nature and My supreme dominion over all that be." (Bg. 9.11) Of course, it is fashionable for certain cheaters to claim to be God, or to "become God" by practicing yoga. But one does not become God. God is always God, changeless and supreme. He is the transcendent reality, both within and beyond the creation. He has no cause. He is fully conscious of everything both directly and indirectly. His name is Krishna, and He has hundreds and thousands of other names.

When Lord Krishna appeared on this earth five thousand years ago, He enacted many wonderful pastimes beyond the scope of any human being. He did not practice yoga to become God. Mother Yasoda even saw the entire universe contained within infant Krishna's mouth. As a child, He lifted Govardhan Hill to protect the inhabitants of Vrindaban against the torrents of rain sent by Indra. From the moment of His appearance, He exhibited His power as the supreme controller. No one is greater than God, nor can anyone be equal to Him. When we understand this, and realize that we are part and parcel of Him, we want to surrender to Him and become His loving servant.

Question: When Lord Krishna walked the earth, He was not accepted as God by everyone. How is an incarnation recognized, or determined?

Srila Bhaktipada: In the Vedas, there are descriptions of various incarnations—Rama, Nrisingha, Varaha, Matsya, Krishna, Balarama, Buddha, Lord Chaitanya, and Kalki—in which the Lord's appearance and mission are disclosed. Even in the Bible, there is a description of the coming of Christ: He would be born of a virgin, He would appear at a certain time and place, and He would preach in a certain way. Therefore to understand the descent of God into the world, we must consult bona fide scripture. No one should be accepted as an avatar without reference to scripture.

Question: Most people today have difficulty accepting the virgin birth of Christ. How is such a doctrine to be understood?

Srila Bhaktipada: Certainly, from the mundane point of view, the virgin birth is very difficult to accept, but by it, we begin to see how spiritual science differs from material science. Although we have no experience of a virgin birth, we must admit that our experience is limited. Even within this material world, an almost unlimited world exists; therefore things outside our realm of experience are always possible.

What then shall we say of the spiritual world, which is far beyond the range of the mind and senses? Transcendental knowledge must be received from a higher authority, a perfect source that is not material and fallible. Unless we receive knowledge from a perfect source, our conclusions will always be imperfect. To err is human. We cannot arrive at universal truth by inductive reasoning, nor by laboratory experiments. Therefore in every developed culture, scriptures are given by God to impart higher knowledge. It is significant that in all of these scriptures, supernatural occurrences, or miracles, appear. A miracle, after all, is just something beyond our common experience. Such miracles are not even necessarily spiritual. By manipulating subtle forces, for instance, yogis can walk on water, fly in the air, create a planet, and so on, and because these are supramundane, or beyond our ordinary, daily experiences, they are taken as miracles. But in truth, Lord Krishna is performing much greater miracles before our eyes daily.

Every day, the great sun rises and sets, and this earth, floating in space, rotates according to infallible laws. Every year, the seasons follow in perfect succession, and in the course of time, all the variegated life on this planet comes into existence, stays for a while, and vanishes. These are all great miracles, operating under the laws of God. If we do not see them as such, it is because our sense of the miraculous has been dulled. This, of course, is our misfortune. "A wicked and adulterous generation seeketh after a sign." (Matt 16.4) We do not have the eyes to see God, nor understand His laws, nor appreciate His great miracles of existence. God and His laws are nondifferent. The laws themselves are miraculous, but due to our dullness, we require that they be contradicted, or suspended, as in the case of the virgin birth. This blindness on our part must be corrected.

Understanding God is therefore the first necessity. First, we must understand that God is omnipotent. He can do whatever He wants. If He wants, He can impregnate a virgin. Why not? For Him, nothing is difficult, nothing impossible. Otherwise, what does it mean to be God?

Question: Scientifically speaking, a virgin birth would certainly be a miracle. Is there any parallel in the Vedic literatures?

Srila Bhaktipada: Yes, many. Lord Krishna's birth is always miraculous. For instance, when Lord Krishna was born to Mother Devaki, He appeared outside her womb in His four-handed Vishnu form. But when Mother Devaki saw this, she was frightened. She was in a very precarious situation because her brother Kamsa, having been told that her eighth child would kill him, had killed all her previous children. Therefore, when she saw this four-armed form, she thought, "Oh, Kamsa will know that the Lord has taken birth here, and he will immediately kill Him." Of course, no one can kill God, but Mother Devaki was thinking in this way. She therefore prayed to the Lord, "Please come as an ordinary child." And, to fulfill His mother's desire, Krishna appeared in His two-armed form.

The birth of Lord Chaitanya was also extraordinary. When He was born, there were wonderful celestial displays, including a full lunar eclipse. At the time, everyone was bathing in the holy rivers and chanting the names of God. From material calculations, it is certainly miraculous to appear at such a moment, but nothing is miraculous for God.

Lord Brahma was even born without a mother. He appeared from a lotus flower that grew directly out of the navel of Lord Vishnu. And Lord Shiva was born directly from Lord Brahma's forehead. When we study the appearances of higher living entities such as the demigods, we often find these uncommon occurrences. Of course, the appearance of the Supreme Personality of Godhead Himself, by His inconceivable potencies, is most important and auspicious. Therefore Lord Krishna says, "He who knows the transcendental nature of My appearance and activities does not, upon leaving the body, take his birth again in this material world, but attains My eternal abode." (Bg. 4.9) Just by understanding the transcendental, supramundane nature of the Lord's appearance, we can attain the Kingdom of God.

Question: Would you explain more about the nature of that appearance and how it differs from ours?

Srila Bhaktipada: God does not come into this world the way we do. Actually, we don't want to take birth, but we are forced to by our past karma. According to our activities in our past life, material nature says, "Change bodies. Now become a dog." Or, "Become a man again." Or, "Become a demigod." In any case, as long as we take a material body—be it that of an ant or the demigod Brahma—we are forced to grow old, suffer disease, and die. Everyone in the material world is forced to suffer these miseries. But God does not. God is not forced to take His birth according to His past karma, nor to take birth in a certain country under certain conditions. No. When He appears, He appears by His own internal energy, according to His own sweet will.

In other words, God appears when and where He likes, and in whatever form He likes. He is never subject to the modes of material nature. His body is always wholly spiritual, *sat-chit-ananda*, eternal, full of knowledge and bliss. Everything is enacted by His own desire. After all, He controls everything. "This material nature is working under My direction," He says (Bg. 9.10). We are controlled by material nature, but Krishna controls nature. He appears for His own purpose, which is infallibly accomplished.

By understanding the transcendental nature of God's appearance, we can begin to understand His greatness. God is the greatest. No one is equal to Him, nor is anyone greater. That is the Vedic conclusion. He is the Supreme Living Entity who maintains all other living entities. When we begin to realize God's greatness, it becomes natural to surrender to Him. Eventually, everyone must surrender to God, but surrender out of love is one thing, and surrender out of fear or out of force is quite another. The more we understand His wonderful qualities—His infinite goodness, beauty, power, fame, wealth, knowledge, and renunciation—the more we will love Him and surrender to Him.

Question: Then God can appear in any way, through a virgin or any other medium?

Srila Bhaktipada: God can do whatever He likes. This it what it means to be God. If He is forced to take birth in a particular way, then how is He God? God means the supreme controller, the cause of all causes. Whatever laws exist are laws only because God has made them laws. So-called universal laws are just expressions of His will, His desire. Of course, this is hard for materialists or atheists to understand. They think that material nature is supreme. In describing the demoniac, Lord Krishna says: "They say that this world is unreal, that there is no foundation, and that there is no God in control. It is produced of sex desire, and has no cause other than lust." (Bg. 16.8) Materialists are unaware of the controller behind material nature. They never ask, "Whose nature is this? Who created it?" For them, sex is the cause of everything. Therefore they scoff at the very mention of a virgin birth, or God's appearance in the world.

God's pure devotees see everything as coming from God. They see His hand in everything. Jesus Christ warned us against materialistic thinking when He said, "Man shall not live by bread alone, but by every word that proceedeth out of the mouth of God." (Matt 4.4) Similarly, St. John spoke of the sons of God as being "born not of blood nor of the will of the flesh, nor of the will of man, but of God." (John 2.13) Since the devotees see everything existing by God's will, they cultivate a very wonderful loving relationship with God. Seeing God as their friend, their child, or their lover, they always relate to Him in transcendental love, and God reciprocates. "As men surrender unto Me," Krishna says, "I reward them accordingly." (Bg. 4.11) If we take one small step toward God, He will take one step toward us. But what is the size of His step? We cannot imagine. In His incarnation as Vamana, He covered the whole universe with a single step. Even though we offer God something insignificant, He gives us so much in return. After all, He has given us the very breath of life.

Question: But what modern scientist would ever admit the appearance of God in the world?

Srila Bhaktipada: Truth is truth, regardless of whether anyone believes it. After all, ignorant people warned Columbus that if he sailed too far, he would fall off the edge of the earth. But Columbus was well aware that the earth is a sphere. Whether scientists believe in God or not doesn't change the facts. The question is, "Does an omnipotent God exist?" If we affirm it, we get one result, and if we deny it, we get another. By believing in a Supreme God and following His word, we can develop a favorable relationship with God and at death go back to Godhead. Or, if we choose to deny Him, we lose the opportunity afforded by human life and continue the process of transmigration through 8,400,000 species of existence.

Question: Could you give us some other example of nature's laws being deliberately contradicted or suspended by God?

Srila Bhaktipada: Well, everything God does is deliberate because He isn't forced to do anything. Nothing is accidental. Because God is the creator of material nature, we can't properly say that He abides by nature's laws or contradicts them. His will *is* nature's law.

When God appears, He enacts many miraculous pastimes. Lord Ramachandra floated huge stones on the ocean to make a bridge from the tip of India to the island of Sri Lanka. The floating of those stones on water appeared miraculous, but no more so than God's floating all these great planets in space. Trying to explain such events is like digging a hole and filling it back up. Our questions dig the hole, and our answers fill it up. This reminds me of Gertrude Stein's dying words: "What is the answer?" she was asked. "In that case," she replied, "what is the question?"

We may describe what is, but never why it is. The answer to all questions is the same: God is omnipotent. He does whatever He wants. Things happen because He wants them to happen. Therefore it is said that one who knows Krishna, or God, knows everything.

Question: Then if we accept the miracles of Christ, we should accept His virgin birth as well?

Srila Bhaktipada: Why not? The virgin birth is no more miraculous than any of God's other pastimes. All of God's activities are wonderful. That is His nature: wonderful. Lord Krishna lifted Govardhan Hill and held it up with His little finger for a whole week, using it as an umbrella to protect all the inhabitants of Vrindaban from the torrential rains sent by Indra. He did this just as easily as a little child might snatch a mushroom and hold it up. God can do anything—that's the point. Why call ourselves devotees, Christians, Hindus, or Muslims, if we don't believe in the inconceivable potencies of God? If God is not transcendental to the laws of material nature, what good is He? If He is controlled by nature, what kind of God is He? Obviously we are controlled by nature. Birth, old age, disease, and death are there whether we want them or not, reminding us that we are fully controlled. But if God is also controlled, how can He help us? Of course, God is not controlled. He controls all others, but He Himself is eternally free. Therefore He can save us.

Question: Freudians suggest that the impregnation of the Virgin Mary by the Holy Spirit in the form of a dove is simply a recurrence of the Greek myth of Leda, who was impregnated by Zeus in the form of a swan. For them, these are only symbols out of man's subconscious, expressions of certain repressed thoughts and desires. What is your answer to this?

Srila Bhaktipada: Freudians may think in this way, but we accept the Vedas and other authorized scriptures as factual. After all, Freud and his followers are all conditioned souls trying to acquire knowledge by the empiric method of mental speculation. But when we accept the word of God, we receive perfect knowledge. Perfect knowledge cannot come from mental speculation, experimentation, or research. It must come from a perfect source. God Himself is perfect, and He is the source of everything; therefore knowledge received from God is perfect.

Because we are human, we are imperfect. But we can receive knowledge from a perfect source and transmit it to others. A child may learn from a mathematician that two plus two equals four, and although he may not understand how this can be, he can repeat this knowledge to other children, and they can benefit. It is truth no matter who says it. When we receive knowledge from the perfect source, that knowledge will act, even though we are imperfect instruments. Knowledge received from God can deliver us from this material world of birth and death. It acts wonderfully because God is wonderful.

Question: Perhaps influenced by the Freudians, some Catholic priests today are saying that it isn't necessary to believe literally in the virgin birth. How would you answer them?

Srila Bhaktipada: Well, maybe they should take up another profession. Today, some so-called theologians are claiming that God is dead. He may be dead for them, but He is alive and well for His devotees. Such people don't realize that we have to qualify ourselves to see God. How is that? That qualification is mentioned in *Brahma-samhita:* "I worship the primeval Lord, Govinda, who is always seen by the devotee whose eyes are anointed with the pulp of love. He is seen in His eternal form of Syamasundara situated within the heart of the devotee." (Bs. 5.38)

He is seen in His real form, just as I am seeing you, or you are seeing me. But God cannot be forced to reveal Himself to us. After all, who are we to demand God to appear before us? We can't even demand this of the president or prime minister. Although God is far away in His eternal abode, He is everywhere, within and between every atom. Just as the sun is present all over the earth in the form of sunshine, God is present throughout His creation in His various energies. His devotees can see Him everywhere. But He cannot be seen by envious materialists, who, in their delusion, want to exploit everything for sense gratification. As I said before, we are not the controllers but the controlled. Only God is the controller, the supreme dominator of all that be.

Question: Could you speak of some of the other incarnations mentioned in the Vedic scriptures?

Srila Bhaktipada: Of course, we are most familiar with Krishna, but millions of years ago God appeared as Lord Ramachandra and displayed the powers of God as an ideal king. These pastimes are narrated by Valmiki in the *Ramayana*. Sometimes the Lord incarnates in other species: as Matsya, the fish incarnation, He preserved the Vedas during the great flood; as Varaha, the boar, He rescued the earth from the Garbha ocean with His tusks; as the tortoise incarnation, He served as the pivot for the churning of the ocean;

as Nrisingha, half-lion half-man, He saved His devotee
Prahlada from the demon Hiranyakashipu.

Question: You also said that Buddha is mentioned?

Srila Bhaktipada: Yes, God incarnated as Lord Buddha to
put an end to animal sacrifice and delude the atheists. Although *Srimad-Bhagavatam* was written more than two
thousand years before Buddha's appearance, His birthplace,
family, and mission are all foretold. At the time of Buddha,
people were indiscriminantly slaughtering animals in the
name of Vedic sacrifice, and for this reason, Buddha rejected
the Vedas. Lord Buddha was most compassionate upon all
living entities. Compassion toward all fallen souls is one of
the characteristics of an incarnation. To put an end to animal
slaughter, Buddha rejected the Vedas, and to get the atheists
to listen to Him, He preached atheism, or disguised atheism.
We consider His teachings atheistic because He rejected the
Vedas and did not directly mention God. Still, He delivered
the atheists in a very clever way: He got them to worship
Him. Although no mention of God is made in the Buddhist
Sutras, the Supreme Lord is worshipped in Buddhist temples
in the form of Lord Buddha. In this way, His mission was
fulfilled.

Question: Is Christ mentioned in the Vedas?

Srila Bhaktipada: Not directly, but His mission is mentioned.
He is a *shaktavesha-avatara*, or empowered representative of
God. His coming is, however, foretold in the Old Testament.

Question: Did Krishna Himself give any guideline by which
an incarnation can be recognized?

Srila Bhaktipada: Yes, in the Eleventh Chapter of *Bhagavad-
gita*, Krishna revealed His *virata-rupa*, the universal form.
This is a temporary form manifested within the material world.
In this universal form, we can see everything: the trees are
the hairs of His body; the sun and moon are His eyes; the
rivers are His veins. All living entities are rushing into His
fiery mouths, which are gates of destruction. When the valiant
warrior Arjuna saw this form, he was terrified. In that gigantic

form, Arjuna could see everything created, maintained, and annihilated. He saw God as the supreme controller, and as Time, the destroyer of all the worlds. Although Arjuna was Krishna's friend and was already convinced of Krishna's divinity, he wanted Krishna to exhibit this form just to verify the fact that He is the Supreme Personality of Godhead. That is, Arjuna wanted the form exhibited for those who have only material vision. No one but God can display such a form. So, this serves as a criterion. If some cheater claims to be God, we can request, "Dear sir, will you please display your universal form to confirm that you are the supreme controller and that everything is working under your direction?"

Question: Since God is always present in everyone's heart as the Supersoul, why does He incarnate? What are the general functions of an avatar?

Srila Bhaktipada: According to *Bhagavad-gita*, there are several reasons. One is to rid the world of miscreants, who rebel against God's authority and create disturbances for God's devotees. Therefore, when Krishna comes to earth, He kills many demons. Another reason is to reestablish religious principles. Forgetfulness is a disease of the conditioned soul, and men tend to forget the principles of religion in the course of time. Only God can establish such principles; therefore Krishna spoke *Bhagavad-gita* on the battlefield of Kurukshetra. Millions of years before, He had spoken it to the sun god Vivasvan, but the chain of disciplic succession was broken and the knowledge lost. Therefore He spoke it again.

Most important, God comes in order to give pleasure to His devotees. The pastimes of the Lord are so wonderful that the devotees become enlivened just by seeing the Lord's transcendental features. Actually, this is the only reason the Lord comes. He can annihilate the miscreants through the agency of His material energy, Mayadevi. And He can reiterate the dharma by means of His devotees such as Vyasadeva or Sukadeva. But only He Himself, in His eternal transcendental personal form, can give pleasure to His devotees.

Question: Can we expect God to appear in the future in some marvelous way?

Srila Bhaktipada: Yes, according to the Vedic literatures, He will appear at the end of this age as the avatar Kalki to destroy all the ungodly and establish the golden age, called Satya-yuga. This will be more than 400,000 years from now, but we don't have to look so far into the future. God is now appearing in a very wonderful way: incarnating in the sounds of His holy names. There is no difference between God and His names. This chanting of Hare Krishna, Hare Krishna, Krishna Krishna, Hare Hare, Hare Rama, Hare Rama, Rama Rama, Hare Hare is spreading all over the world. Here is Lord Chaitanya's inconceivable potency at work. It is so powerful that it will interrupt Kali-yuga, this age of ignorance and quarrel, and usher in a golden age of God consciousness for the next ten thousand years. As Lord Krishna says: "Whenever and wherever there is a decline in religious practice and a predominant rise of irreligion—at that time, I descend Myself. In order to deliver the pious and to annihilate the miscreants, as well as to reestablish the principles of religion, I Myself appear, millennium after millennium." (Bg. 4.7-8) It has already begun.

God's wonders never cease. He is eternally wonderful. In the past, He displayed many wonderful pastimes; at present, He is acting wonderfully; and in the future, the devotees will live with Him in the eternal Kingdom of God, where all His wonderful pastimes are eternally manifest. He is calling us now to come and join Him in this wonderful life of Krishna consciousness and spread the chanting of His holy name to every town and village of the world. Hare Krishna.

CHAPTER FIVE

Chanting The Names Of God

Question: Why do you chant Hare Krishna all the time?

Srila Bhaktipada: Chanting is the best means for remembering the Lord, especially in this age. In fact, chanting is called the *yuga-dharma*, the way to salvation in this very difficult age of Kali, an age of ignorance and quarrel. Who can deny that chanting is a very practical method for everyone? If you don't like the name Krishna, you can chant whatever bona fide name of God you prefer. You can continue to be a Christian, Muslim, or Buddhist. You don't have to qualify before some examining board. You don't have to be educated or rich. Chanting doesn't cost anything, and it can be done anytime, anyplace. There are no material impediments. Anyone can chant the names of the Lord and receive the highest benefit.

Question: What do you mean when you say that Krishna and His names are nondifferent?

Srila Bhaktipada: Because God is absolute, He is not different from His names. In this relative material world, everything depends on something else. My existence depends on my father, and his existence depends on his father, but God is the original Father, the cause of all causes. His existence depends on nothing outside Himself. There is no difference between Krishna and Krishna's form, nor between Krishna and His name, nor between Krishna and His activities. In the material world, there is a difference between a word and its referent. If we chant, "Water, water," we will continue to be thirsty. But God's name is not like this. If we chant God's names, we can immediately feel the Lord's presence. This is due to God's absolute nature. God and anything relating to God is the same. His names therefore are filled with spiritual potency. They are God incarnate in sound.

Question: Would you explain the words of the Hare Krishna mantra?

Srila Bhaktipada: "Hare" refers to the Lord's energy; "Krishna" refers to the all-attractive Lord Himself; and "Rama" refers to the Lord as the supreme enjoyer. These words, placed in order, constitute a sixteen word mantra: Hare Krishna, Hare Krishna, Krishna Krishna, Hare Hare, Hare Rama, Hare Rama, Rama Rama, Hare Hare. The word "mantra" means "mind delivering," and this Hare Krishna mantra is often called the *maha-mantra*, or great mantra for deliverance from the cycle of birth and death.

Because we cannot see the Lord at the present moment, we have to approach Him by His energy, which we can see and feel. Although God is everywhere, we need spiritual vision to see Him, and God has made Himself easily available to all through His holy names. "Hare" invokes that self-revealing energy. The word "Krishna" specifically denotes the reservoir of all opulences, the all-attractive Lord who possesses unlimited wealth, fame, beauty, knowledge, strength, and renunciation. All people are naturally attracted by these opulences, for God is their fountainhead. "Rama" refers to God as enjoyer of everything. Because we are part and parcel of God, it is our nature to enjoy also, but being finite, we cannot enjoy independently or unlimitedly. God can, however. Everything is meant for His enjoyment, including us. When we learn how to serve the Lord for His enjoyment, we fulfill the real purpose of life.

Question: Is chanting recommended in the Bible?

Srila Bhaktipada: Yes, in many places. In both the Old and New Testaments, there is frequent reference to the spiritual potency of God's name. Moses spoke of "singing unto the Lord, for He hath triumphed gloriously." (Exodus 15.1) Also: "Thou shalt fear the Lord thy God; Him shalt thou serve, and to Him shalt thou cleave, and swear by His name." (Deut 10.20) And: "I will publish the name of the Lord; ascribe ye greatness unto our God." (Deut 32.3) Although the Jewish scribes would not write the holy name, they indicated it in other ways. The Psalmist in numerous passages exhorted all to sing and glorify the holy names. "All nations whom Thou hast made shall come and worship before Thee, O Lord; and shall glorify Thy name." (Psalms 86.9) Also: "Give thanks unto the Lord, call upon His name, make known His deeds among the people. Sing unto Him, sing ye psalms unto Him, talk yet of all His wondrous works. Glory ye in His holy name." (I Chron 16.8-10)

In the New Testament, St. Paul advises: "For whosoever shall call upon the name of the Lord shall be saved." (Romans 10.13)) When Christ told His disciples to go forth and preach among all men that "The kingdom of God is come nigh unto you," (Luke 10.9) He was essentially telling them to spread kirtan, or God-praise. Whether one says, "Repent, the Kingdom of God is at hand,"or chants Hare Krishna, the message is basically the same. Christ may not have chanted Hare Krishna , but He did say, "For where two or three are gathered together in my name, there am I in the midst of them." (Matt 18.20) He also said, "O Father...I have manifested Thy name unto the men which Thou gavest me out of the world....Holy Father, keep through Thine own name those whom Thou hast given me, that they may be one as we are. While I was with them in the world I kept them in Thy name...." (John 17.6,11-12) And He taught us to pray: "Our Father, which art in heaven, hallowed be Thy name." (Matt 6.9)

Calling upon God's name has always been recognized as authorized and effective. We do not say that only the Hare Krishna *maha-mantra* can be chanted. Any bona fide name of God is spiritual, and by chanting it, we become spiritualized. When we contact electricity, we become electrified, regardless of the medium carrying the electricity. The understanding should be that God's name is not material but spiritual and nondifferent from Him. That is taught in every scripture. In the Christian tradition, the Church fathers particularly stressed chanting the names of God. This comes down to us in the Catholic tradition of the rosary, and in the Gregorian chants and Protestant hymns, which were frequently sung in a "Church of the Holy Name."

Question: Then could a Christian chant, "Jesus, Jesus"?

Srila Bhaktipada: Certainly. The Jesus Prayer is sometimes chanted: "Lord Jesus Christ, have mercy on me." Any bona fide name for the Lord can be chanted. As Lord Chaitanya says, "My dear Lord, You have hundreds and thousands of names, and in them You have invested all Your transcendental potencies. You have kindly made it easy to approach You by chanting Your holy names, but I am so unfortunate that I have no attraction for them." (*Sikshastakam*)

God is unlimited and is called by an unlimited number of names throughout His creation. Even we, limited as we are, often have more than one name. "Father calls me William, sister calls me Will, mother calls me Willie, but the fellers call me Bill." According to how well a person knows us, he may call us by a more or less intimate name. A lover may have a name for his beloved that no one else knows. Similarly, some of God's names are more intimate than others.

As the devotee develops pure love for God, he comes to know more and more about the Lord and His names. Krishna is a very intimate name, as is Govinda, which refers specifically to Krishna's pastimes with the cows. In Sanskrit, the word *go* means "cow" as well as "senses." The Lord gives pleasure both to the cows and the senses. Materialists are always trying to satisfy their senses with gross sense objects, but only Lord Govinda can satisfy the senses fully. Every morning, in temples throughout India, the *Vishnu-sahasranam*, the "thousand names of God," are chanted. And in the Christian tradition, in the Catholic litanies, the many attributes of God are chanted: "Wonderful, Counselor, Everlasting Father, Prince of Peace." So all facilities are there. We simply have to put them to use.

Question: What are some of the guidelines for chanting, and who sets them?

Srila Bhaktipada: The Lord Himself. He is the author of religion, and He alone sets down religious principles. "Real religious principles are enacted by the Supreme Personality of Godhead. Although fully situated in the mode of goodness, even the great rishis who occupy the topmost planets cannot ascertain the real religious principles, nor can the demigods, nor the leaders of Siddhaloka, to say nothing of the demons, ordinary human beings, Vidyadharas and Caranas." (*Srimad-Bhagavatam* 6.3.19)

We cannot make up something and say, "Well, I think this is what religion ought to be." The most important religious principle, enunciated by Lord Krishna Himself in every chapter of *Bhagavad-gita*, is surrender to God. Surrender is the symptom of our love. When one loves, he surrenders. If we want to develop love of God, we have to surrender to Him. To this end, the Lord Himself instructs us to perform sacrifice in everything we do: "All that you do, all that you eat, all that you offer and give away, as well as all austerities that you may perform, should be done as an offering unto Me." (Bg. 9.27)

When chanting, we have to follow the Lord's instructions. We shouldn't chant whimsically, or for personal benefit. For instance, in the scriptures it is stated that by chanting the Lord's holy names, we counteract the effects of all sinful activities. But it is offensive to think, "Oh, I can go out and sin all week. Then on Sunday morning I'll chant God's names and counteract all sinful reactions." This cheating mentality will never help us. If we are truly experiencing the Lord's mercy by chanting His holy names, how can we continue sinning? We must be sincere. If we love the Lord, we have to follow His instructions. "If ye love me, keep my commandments," Christ said (John 14.15).

The very word "disciple" means one who follows a discipline. We have to accept the discipline of the spiritual master, and in this way, show our love. In order to be effective, chanting must be done attentively, with a humble and sincere heart. We have to want to surrender to God and love Him with all our heart. We should chant just like a helpless child calling to his father: "My dear Lord, please help me. Please pick me up from this ocean of birth and death, and engage me in Your devotional service." This should be our attitude. The Lord will never disappoint us.

Question: Some gurus have secret or private mantras. They charge their disciples money for the mantra and then tell them to keep it a secret. Why is Hare Krishna for everyone, and free as well?

Srila Bhaktipada: Long ago, when the great devotee Ramanujacarya received the Hare Krishna mantra, his spiritual master told him, "This is the most powerful mantra. It will eradicate all your sins and liberate you from the cycle of birth and death. Chant it, but don't tell it to anyone." Despite this warning, Ramanujacarya immediately went out into the street and proclaimed to everyone: "Chant this Hare Krishna mantra. It is the most powerful mantra. It will relieve you of all sins." When his spiritual master heard about this, he called Ramanujacarya before him and said, "I told you not to tell this mantra to anyone. Why have you disobeyed me?" "Yes, I understood your instructions," Ramanujacarya said, "but when you told me that this mantra could liberate everyone, I had no other recourse. I had to tell everyone. You can send me to hell, or do with me as you like, but I had to deliver them." Then his spiritual master said, "Actually, you are a great devotee. You have truly understood the importance of Hare Krishna."

Why should something so wonderful be kept a secret? If it can liberate anyone from the cycle of birth and death, how can we not proclaim it? How can we charge money for it? No. It is proclaimed publicly and given freely. It brings the greatest benefit and the greatest benediction. But we should not think that, because it is free, it is cheap or worthless. No. It is more valuable than God's free sunshine. God Himself is giving it freely, out of love for us. He is giving Himself in the form of His name. How can there be a price? How could we ever give anything in exchange for Him? But there is a responsibility entailed. When the Lord's mercy is freely given to us, we have to give up sinful activity and distribute the mercy to others.

Question: How long do the devotees chant each day?

Srila Bhaktipada: Actually a devotee should chant constantly. But there is a required daily chanting of a minimum of sixteen rounds on beads. This is called *japa*. There are 108 beads on a *japa-mala* (string of beads), and on each bead we chant the complete *maha-mantra* once—that is, Hare Krishna, Hare Krishna, Krishna Krishna, Hare Hare, Hare Rama, Hare Rama, Rama Rama, Hare Hare. If we chant sixteen rounds, we are chanting about 25,000 holy names. This takes about an hour and a half, or two hours at most. This much is required of all initiated devotees. Apart from this, a devotee is always mentally repeating Hare Krishna, no matter what he's doing—cleaning, cooking, working in the fields. This is also chanting.

Question: Does this chanting ever become hackneyed or tiresome?

Srila Bhaktipada: No, because it is spiritual. In this material world, things become old or hackneyed because they are influenced by time. Popular songs, for instance, are popular for only a few weeks. Then their popularity diminishes because people get tired of hearing them. They become hackneyed. But since the Lord's holy names are spiritual, they are not under the influence of time. We can chant these names forever, and they will remain fresh. That is one of the qualities of Krishna—ever fresh. Even though He had been on this earth 125 years when He spoke *Bhagavad-gita* on the battlefield of Kurukshetra, He appeared just like a fresh youth. His body is eternal and spiritual, and never deteriorates like ours. Similarly, His name remains ever new and fresh. We can chant it forever. Its beauty increases eternally.

Question: What effect does chanting have on the mind?

Srila Bhaktipada: It soothes the mind because it is identical with Krishna. Krishna is our best friend and the Prince of Peace. By His name, He can give peace to our mind. That is the meaning of the Sanskrit word *shantih:* perfect, unshakable peace, beyond the experience of this material world.

Question: Has anyone ever gone insane from chanting?

Srila Bhaktipada: No, but many have from not chanting. The greatest teachers, philosophers, and intellectuals have been chanters of the Lord's holy names. In India, the great *acharyas* and spiritual masters have always chanted. They wrote many treatises on spiritual life and influenced the masses. Were they insane? If their brains became soft from chanting, how could they have been great leaders? Mohandas Gandhi regularly chanted. Was he mad, or defective?

Question: Are there any material benefits from chanting?

Srila Bhaktipada: Chanting will save you money and time because it will allow you to control your senses. Just consider how much money we throw away trying to satisfy the unnecessary desires of the senses. People spend money in restaurants because they cannot control their tongues, or at movies because they cannot control their eyes. They waste their resources on intoxication, prostitution, gambling, meat-eating, and so much else, simply because their senses are demanding satisfaction. But the senses are insatiable. They can never be satisfied by any amount of material sense gratification. Unlimited enjoyment can come only from the sound of the names of God. The senses don't need anything else.

Question: Can any physical or medical benefits be acquired by chanting?

Srila Bhaktipada: Yes. Chanting releases tension caused by worry, disperses anxiety, rests the mind, and lowers the blood pressure. Many other material benefits have also been proved by clinical study. And recently I read that a physician from

Kent, Ohio, has discovered that chanting integrates the two sides of the brain. Meditation and other religious practices can also do this, but chanting was specifically mentioned. It is, moreover, the recommended process for this age.

Of course, we don't advocate such material reasons for chanting. After all, material benefits are temporary, whereas spiritual benefits are eternal. The real purpose is to increase our love of God. Therefore we simply request: "Chant God's names. If you have no specific name for God, then join us in chanting Hare Krishna." It is both easy and sublime.

CHAPTER SIX
Understanding Scripture

Question: First of all, how would you define scripture?

Srila Bhaktipada: Scripture means the word of God. Because we are trying to get back to the Kingdom of God from this material world, we require directions. There are many different scriptures, given at different times and places, to direct mankind back to Godhead. The Christians have the Bible; the Hindus, the Vedas; the Moslems, the Koran; and the Buddhists, the Sutras. In any case, the essential principle is that scripture be inspired by God or spoken by God. The Bible tells us that "holy men of God spoke as they were moved by the Holy Ghost." (2 Peter 1.21) *Bhagavad-gita* is scripture because it was spoken by Lord Krishna, God Himself, to His devotee Arjuna. In any case, scripture must be spoken by God or by a pure devotee who is free from the defects of conditioned souls.

Ordinary human beings are subject to four basic defects. First, our senses are obviously imperfect. Since we cannot claim to hear everything or see everything, our knowledge must be imperfect. Perfection can come only from perfection, and imperfection can beget only imperfection. The opinions or speculations of another human being, subject to the defects of conditioned and imperfect senses, cannot help us attain the Kingdom of God, which is beyond the senses. Second, we have the tendency to commit mistakes. "To err is human." That is our frail human nature. Even the greatest of men make mistakes from time to time. Sometimes, as in the case of Kennedy or Gandhi, these mistakes are fatal. Third, we tend to be illusioned. Because these bodies are born in a certain country at a certain time, we tend to be mistaken about our identity, and we think, "I am this body." How can a person who is under illusion possibly have perfect knowledge? The poet Blake once wrote:

> This life's dim windows of the soul
> Distorts the heavens from pole to pole
> And leads you to believe a lie
> When you see with, not through, the eye.

As long as we believe the lie that we are this body, and as long as our knowledge is acquired "with, not through" these defective senses, we are illusioned. We cannot have perfect knowledge, nor can we give perfect directions.

And fourth, every conditioned soul has the tendency to cheat. Even though we make mistakes, have imperfect senses, and are illusioned, we assume the part of perfect master and thus cheat others. If someone praises us, saying, "You are a great person," we do not disagree. Indeed, we cheat even up to the point of claiming, "I am God." There are many rascals who proclaim themselves to be incarnations. As if God were so cheap! This is simply the cheating tendency at work. Therefore this world has been called the habitation of cheaters and cheated.

Even in mundane life, an ordinary citizen cannot go out in the streets and proclaim his own laws. Who would listen to him? To be recognized as valid, laws must be instituted by the government, and must pass through the proper legislative channels. Similarly, the laws of God must come from the authoritative source, God Himself.

Question: Some people maintain that after many generations, scriptures arise out of sophisticated cultures, that they embody the religious yearnings of peoples, or that they are composed by priests and holymen. What is your view of this?

Srila Bhaktipada: How can God's book of laws be a product of human culture? If you violate these laws, you suffer. For instance, according to material laws, if you do not eat properly, you become sickly. Such laws may be described by scientists, but scientists cannot make the laws. The laws are set down by material nature, which is working under God's direction. Being the ultimate lawgiver, God is the author of all bona fide scripture. In *Bhagavad-gita*, Lord Krishna states: "By all the Vedas am I to be known; indeed, I am the compiler of Vedanta, and I am the knower of the Vedas." (Bg. 15.15)

As long as we continue violating the laws of God, thereby separating ourselves from God, we exclude ourselves from God's Kingdom, and we suffer. Factually, we are in this material world because we have violated God's laws. This entire material universe is a prison where those who have violated God's laws are shackled by the three modes of material nature. Our cells may be first class, second class, or third class, but we are all prisoners. Moreover, we are controlled by lust, anger, and greed, which force us to take birth again and again according to karma. If we want to get free of this prisonhouse and its cycle of birth and death, we have to learn to abide by the laws of God.

This means accepting the scriptures, or the instructions of God from His representative, and thus surrendering to Him. All bona fide scriptures point to this surrender because it relieves us of all misery and fear. Fear is due to forgetting God and identifying with the material body. Since the soul is eternal, we are not subject to death, but without this knowledge, we are always in fear, thinking, "I am going to die." Scripture is God's word given to relieve this fear. It is not given for our harassment but for our correction, enlightenment, and ultimate happiness. By following scripture, we reestablish our loving relationship with God and become fearless.

Question: Then the Koran, for example, would be considered scripture, but not the Dialogues of Plato?

Srila Bhaktipada: Yes, that's one example. The Dialogues of Plato may contain some truths about life, or some observations about the soul, but the Socratic method is essentially one of mental speculation. These are the reasonings or opinions of a conditioned soul, and as such they cannot give us factual information of the Kingdom of God, nor of the laws of God, nor of the means whereby we can reestablish our loving relationship with God. The Koran, however, is spoken by a prophet of God. It deals exclusively with God and teaches men how to surrender to God. That is the principle of all genuine scripture.

Question: But can't the Platonic dialogues treat the truth just as profoundly? Who determines whether Mohammed or Socrates delivered the word of God?

Srila Bhaktipada: Neither Plato nor Socrates ever claims to be a prophet or representative of God. Nor do they claim to be divinely inspired by God, nor their dialogues to be scripture handed down by God. The prophet Mohammed, however, does. Similarly, Christ says that He is "the Word," and "the Way, the Truth, and the Light." And Lord Krishna directly states that He is God Himself: "I am the source of all spiritual and material worlds. Everything emanates from Me." (Bg. 10.8) Moreover, who can deny the extraordinary effects of their teachings? Over the centuries, they have inspired millions of people to dedicate their lives to God and surrender to Him.

Question: Protestants believe in individual interpretation of the Bible, or "the still small voice within," whereas the Catholics maintain that the Church or the Pope is the ultimate interpreter. Which view would you support?

Srila Bhaktipada: As long as we are conditioned souls, we cannot interpret scriptures for ourselves. I've already mentioned that the conditioned soul is subject to four defects. You speak of the "still small voice," but factually there are many voices within. How can we distinguish whether the voice is that of God, or that of false ego, lust, pride, or greed? Unless a bona fide authority helps us understand scripture, we are sure to be misled. Therefore Lord Krishna Himself says, "Just try to learn the truth by approaching a spiritual master. Inquire from him submissively and render service unto him. The self-realized soul can impart knowledge unto you because he has seen the truth." (Bg. 4.34) To understand the truths of scripture, we need the help of a liberated soul. Can an ordinary citizen interpret the laws of the state for himself? No. The statements of expert lawyers and judges are required.

Question: What if the Pope, or spiritual master, is not self-realized but is a rascal, like the Medici Popes, or certain so-called gurus?

Srila Bhaktipada: Then one will be cheated. Therefore, some preliminary knowledge is required. If I go to the market to buy gold, but have no idea what gold is, I will be cheated. Someone will surely give me fool's gold or some worthless alloy. It is necessary to know how to recognize gold, and how to test its purity. Similarly, we should know the test for God's representative. That is not difficult. The real spiritual master does not direct his disciple to anyone but God Himself. He does not say, "I am God," or "You are God," or "We are all God." No. He says, "God is God, and we are His servants. Surrender to Him." In *Bhagavad-gita*, Krishna, says, "Abandon all varieties of religion and just surrender unto Me. I shall deliver you from all sinful reaction. Do not fear." (Bg. 18.66) The bona fide guru does not contradict this.

Question: Are there any other guidelines for checking whether a guru or spiritual master is teaching the truth?

Srila Bhaktipada: *Guru-sadhu-shastra.* These three are always in accord. In Sanskrit, the scripture is called Shastra, the great holymen throughout history are called sadhus, and one's personal spiritual master is called the guru. When these three are in agreement, we can be certain that this is truth. They form a triangle, which is the most rigid of forms. If a spiritual master agrees with the great holymen and with scripture, he can be accepted as a bona fide representative of God. All scriptures teach surrender to God; and the exemplary lives of great holymen show us how to surrender; and the guru personally directs us to surrender. There is no contradiction.

Question: How can we account for the various interpretations of scripture? Are the scriptures deliberately obscure?

Srila Bhaktipada: No. Why should God be obscure? Is it that He can't express Himself perfectly? God has given the scriptures for our enlightenment, and if they appear obscure, it is due to our deviousness, to our lack of understanding of God's ways. Scripture is very clear to those who have surrendered to God, but obscure to those who are envious of Him. That is God's way of protecting the spiritual truth. Krishna says, "I am never manifest to the foolish and unintelligent. For them, I am covered by My eternal creative potency [*yoga-maya*]; and so the deluded world knows Me not, who am unborn and infallible." (Bg. 7.25)

To understand scripture properly, we must qualify. If we go to a university, we will find that there are prerequisites for certain courses. In order to take History 304, for instance, we first have to take History 101 and 102. Similarly, the prerequisite for understanding scripture is surrender to God. As long as we remain envious of God, thinking that we are God, or can become God, we cannot understand His ways. His scriptures will forever remain obscure or occult.

Question: Some people argue that the "still small voice within" is the Supersoul. If this is the case, why do we need a teacher?

Srila Bhaktipada: As I mentioned before, because we are conditioned souls, subject to four basic defects, we cannot see or hear God directly. Certainly, God is situated within our heart as the *chaitya-guru*, the teacher within, and also as the witness of all our activities. And He is so merciful that He appears externally in the form of the pure devotee, God's representative, and confirms and identifies that voice in the heart. As I said, there are many voices within. We can know which voice is God's because, from without, the guru points to that voice within and says, "Oh, now Krishna is speaking to you in your heart." Then we can understand everything.

Question: How might a guru elucidate a Biblical verse? For instance, "In my Father's house are many mansions." (John 14.2) What would be the Vedic explanation?

Srila Bhaktipada: This can be elucidated in two ways. First, according to *Padma Purana*, there are 8,400,000 species of life—insects, aquatics, birds, beasts, humans, demigods, etc.— and all these are like different apartments in God's house. God does not exclusively love human beings. Krishna says, "I am the Father of all living entities." (Bg. 14.4) God has created everything; He is the author of all creation. For His fragmental parts—the *jivas*, or individual spirit souls—He creates these 8,400,000 apartments, and the soul is placed in one or another according to individual desire and activity.

As for the primary meaning: in the unlimited spiritual sky, or the Kingdom of God, there are innumerable spiritual planets, which we call Vaikuntha planets. The word "Vaikuntha" means "without anxiety." Everything about these planets is *sat-chit-ananda*—eternal and full of knowledge and bliss. On each of them, the Supreme Lord expands Himself in different forms to fulfill the particular desires of His devotees. For instance, among these planets is a planet where Lord Jesus Christ reigns. On another planet, Lord Ramachandra resides. And in Goloka Vrindaban, Lord Krishna Himself sports with His devotees in His original form as Govinda, the cowherd boy. There are countless spiritual planets where God's expansions reside and predominate. Thus there are many mansions in God's great house, the infinite spiritual sky. According to the devotee's particular relationship with the Lord, he goes to a specific abode to associate with the Lord in that mood.

Question: Perhaps you would explain another well known verse: "No man, having put his hand to the plough and looking back, is fit for the Kingdom of God." (Luke 9.62)

Srila Bhaktipada: Interestingly enough, these words of Christ have their counterparts in the Old Testament and the Vedic scriptures. In Genesis, we find that when Lot was given the chance to flee Sodom and Gomorrah, he was told, "Look not behind thee." (Gen 19.17) And when Lot's wife foolishly looked back, she turned into a pillar of salt.

Similarly, in the Vedic tradition, the *Chaitanya-charitamrita* tells of one devotee who asked a Deity of Lord Krishna to accompany him to his village to be a witness to an oath. Even though the Deity was made of stone, He agreed to follow His devotee, on the condition that the devotee not look back at Him. While walking, the devotee could hear the ankle bells of the Deity following him, and when the devotee looked back to see, the Deity immediately stopped and never moved again. The devotee then built a temple for the Deity on that spot, the temple of Sakshi Gopal in present-day Orissa.

In both cases, "looking back" means not having sufficient faith in the Lord. The act of looking back is a turning to the blunt material senses. "Without faith it is impossible to please God," the epistle to the Hebrews states. (Heb 11.6) It is faith that is pleasing to God. We should not try to see God with these material eyes, or try to understand Him by imperfect material reasoning. Our senses are imperfect. If we want to understand God, we have to see through the eye of faith. "Only unto those great souls who have implicit faith in both the Lord and the spiritual master are all the imports of Vedic knowledge automatically revealed." (*Svetasvatara Upanishad*) If we turn back from this sublime life of faith to the garbage of the mundane senses—just as a dog returns to its vomit—we are verily condemned. Still, because we are conditioned to enjoy the material senses, we sometimes look back to the things of this material world, and again hanker for them. We should understand, however, that they are pale and insignificant compared to the wonderful spiritual enjoyment available to God's pure devotees. To look back is a great offense.

Question: Who would you say is presently qualified to teach scripture?

Srila Bhaktipada: Anyone who teaches how to surrender to God. There again, the scriptures inform us that chanting the holy names of God is the easiest and most practical method of surrender in this age. We are most fortunate that Srila Prabhupada brought this method to the Western world. Now we are trying to follow in his footsteps. By always thinking of God, by becoming absorbed in hearing the pastimes of Krishna and chanting His holy names, we naturally develop love for Him and want to surrender. It is at once easy and sublime. Chant Hare Krishna and be happy!

CHAPTER SEVEN

Reincarnation And The Nature Of The Soul

Question: Was reincarnation ever taught in the Christian tradition?

Srila Bhaktipada: Yes. For instance, John the Baptist was asked whether or not he was Elias reincarnated (John 1.21), and although John denied it, Christ Himself said of John, "And if ye will receive it, this is Elias, which was for to come." (Matt. 11.14) And when Christ Himself asked His disciples, "Whom do they say I am?" they replied, "Some say that thou art John the Baptist; some Elias; and others, Jeremias, or one of the prophets." (Matt 16.14) There might have been some disagreement about the previous identity of John or Christ, but these passages indicate that reincarnation was accepted at the time. Christ never denied it. Of course, the transmigration of the soul is elaborately explained in Vedic literature, but we also find that cultures as diverse as the Celts, Indonesians, Druids, pre-Christian Irish, ancient Egyptians, and Greeks accepted it in one form or another. People as simple as the Australian aborigines, or as sophisticated as the psychologist Carl Jung, have accepted it. What is the difficulty?

Although Christ Himself acknowledged transmigration, it is not admitted in the Christian religion because the early Church fathers taught that the human soul is created by God at a certain point in time, and, at death, goes to either heaven or hell for eternity. That is, God breathed a soul into man, and man only. Other life forms, such as plants and animals, have no soul, according to Church fathers such as Augustine and Aquinas. Since the soul of man is a one-shot affair—going to either heaven or hell—there is no question of transmigration. And since animals have no soul, it is all right to kill and eat them. In this way, by interpreting the words of Christ to conform to their own desires, certain Christians have made sure that their sense gratification can continue unchecked.

Question: Often, in the Aristotelian and Christian traditions, the soul is equated with the higher mental processes, and from this it is concluded that animals have no soul. Is the soul identical with the mind?

Srila Bhaktipada: No. The soul is eternal, but the mind is not. Although subtle, the mind is part of the material energy. Krishna says, "Earth, water, fire, air, ether, mind, intelligence, and false ego—altogether these eight comprise My separated material energies. Besides this inferior nature, there is a superior energy of Mine, which is all living entities who are struggling with material nature and sustaining the universe." (Bg. 7.4-5) That living entity (*jiva-bhutam*) is spirit soul.

This gross body, which is composed of earth, water, fire, air, and ether, is born of an earthly father and mother. But the subtle body, composed of mind, intelligence, and false ego, is different. At night, for instance, the subtle body may leave the gross body and travel at will, although remaining connected to the gross body. At death, that connection with the gross body is severed, and the subtle body does not return. With the soul, it enters another mother's womb, where another gross body is provided for that subtle body to express itself. "The living entity in the material world carries his different conceptions of life from one body to another as the air carries aromas. Thus taking another gross body, he obtains a certain type of ear, tongue, and nose and sense of touch, which are grouped about the mind. He thus enjoys a particular set of sense objects." (Bg. 15.8-9) That is, he acquires senses by which to experience sense gratification. This is the process of transmigration, or reincarnation. "As a person puts on new garments, giving up old ones, similarly, the soul accepts new material bodies, giving up the old and useless ones." (Bg. 2.22) We all come into this material world with the desire to enjoy sense gratification. That is the root cause of our conditioning.

Question: What, then, are some of the characteristics of the soul?

Srila Bhaktipada: The soul is superior to the gross and subtle bodies. "The soul is transcendental, eternal, and beyond the modes of nature. Despite contact with the material body, the soul neither does anything nor is entangled. The sky, due to its subtle nature, does not mix with anything, although it is all pervading. Similarly, the soul, situated in Brahman vision, does not mix with the body, though situated in that body. As the sun illuminates this universe, so does the soul, one with the body, illuminate the entire body by consciousness." (Bg. 13.32-33)

This soul is unborn and eternal. "For the soul there is never birth nor death. Nor, having once been, does he ever cease to be. He is unborn, eternal, ever-existing, undying and primeval. He is not slain when the body is slain." (Bg. 2.20) The soul is *sat-chit-ananda:* eternal, full of knowledge and bliss. Due to contact with the material body, he has forgotten his original, pure, *sat-chit-ananda* nature.

We can understand that the soul is present by the presence of consciousness. When consciousness is no longer in the body, the body is dead—whether it is the body of an ant, a dog, or a man. "Oh, he is gone," we say, meaning that the soul is gone. We can see that this is true of all life—including plants, trees, aquatics, insects, birds, and animals—because all living entities have souls. "I think therefore I am." Because we have consciousness, we know that we exist. After all, the body itself is nothing but a bunch of chemicals. If we combine these chemicals, what will happen? Chemicals are inert; they cannot move. They are dead until they come in contact with the soul.

Because the soul is present in the body, the body can move

and feel. We are not the body, not just a bunch of chemicals. That soul, that consciousness, is our real self, our real identity. And if we can understand the soul's presence in ourselves, we can understand its presence in other bodies also. An animal's consciousness may not be as developed as ours, but he also feels pleasure and pain. He is aware of certain things, in fact, many things that we may not be aware of. The animal is also afraid of death. He also must eat, sleep, defend, and mate. How can anyone say that the animal has no consciousness? And since consciousness is the symptom of the soul, the animal certainly has a soul.

Question: What do you mean by the Supersoul?

Srila Bhaktipada: In Sanskrit, the word *atma* refers to the individual soul, which is the knower of one particular body. I may know something of my body, but I don't know anything of yours. Actually, since I don't know everything about my body, I'm an imperfect knower of even my own body.

Paramatma, or the Supersoul, refers to the perfect knower of all bodies—that is, God. "In this body there is another, a transcendental enjoyer who is the Lord, the supreme proprietor, who exists as the overseer and permitter, and who is known as the Supersoul." (Bg. 13.23) The body is called the field of activities, and God is called the knower of all fields, regardless of species. As the Supersoul, God knows what is going on everywhere.

In the Upanishads, the soul and Supersoul are likened to two birds in a tree. The tree is the material body. One bird, the *jiva-atma*, or individual soul, is trying to enjoy the fruits of the tree, which are the objects of the senses. The other bird, the Supersoul, is simply witnessing the activities of His friend. The Lord does not try to enjoy these temporary material bodies, but He accompanies us through our different changes of bodies as the Lord in the heart. Krishna says, "One who sees the Supersoul accompanying the individual soul in all bodies, and who understands that neither the soul nor the Supersoul is ever destroyed, actually sees." (Bg. 13.28) The

Lord is always waiting for us to turn our attention toward Him, but we are so engrossed in trying to enjoy the objects of the senses, that we deny or ignore Him. Of course, sense objects will never give us real happiness. When we finally understand this, we may turn to our eternal Friend, the Supersoul, and discover real, unlimited happiness in His association.

Question: In *Bhagavad-gita*, the soul is said to be an eternal fragment of Krishna. Can you explain this?

Srila Bhaktipada: The Lord is the complete whole; outside of Him, there is nothing. *Srimad-Bhagavatam* says that before the creation, nothing existed but the Lord; during the creation, there is nothing but the Lord; and after annihilation, what remains is the Lord. So in all stages, there is only the Lord. But for His pleasure, the Lord expands Himself into many. The living entities are expansions of the Lord, and in this sense, they are identical with Him, but this does not mean that they are equal to Him. "The living entities in this conditional world are My eternal, fragmental parts. Due to conditioned life, they are struggling very hard with the six senses, which include the mind." (Bg. 15.7)

Sometimes yogis and impersonal Mayavadi philosophers make the mistake of thinking, "I am God." No. We are little fragments of God, part and parcel of God. If we were God, how could we ever become forgetful of our real nature? God does not forget. If He did, forgetfulness would be greater than God. But we can forget by being covered with another energy of God. That covering energy is maya, the power of illusion.

We are one in quality with the Lord, but different in quantity. That quality is spiritual: we are not matter but spirit. Just as God is the Supreme Spirit, we, His fragmental parts, are eternal, individual spirits. From the very beginning of *Bhagavad-gita*, Krishna proclaims the eternal individuality of the soul: "Never was there a time when I did not exist, nor you, nor all these kings; nor in the future shall any of us cease to be." (Bg. 2.12) But we are never equal to God in all ways, not even after liberation.

Everything is existing unlimitedly in the Supreme Personality of Godhead. He is the reservoir of all qualities, and, in the living entity, we find these qualities in minute degrees. As eternal fragments of the Lord, we are always subordinate to Him. Amongst all living entities, He is the supreme living entity who is maintaining all.

Question: Then, is the individual soul essentially the same, whether it's in the body of a dog, cow, or man?

Srila Bhaktipada: Krishna explicitly says that the wise man sees the soul equally in all living beings: "The humble sage, by virtue of true knowledge, sees with equal vision a learned and gentle *brahmana*, a cow, an elephant, a dog, and a dog-eater." (Bg. 5.18) The same part and parcel of God is there, regardless of the body, and regardless of the theorizing of these so-called philosophers who are trying to justify animal slaughter. The soul is the same; the body changes. After all, the body is received due to previous activities. This body is like a dress, which is changed from time to time. By seeing the body, we can understand something of the soul's karma. We come into this world to fulfill certain desires, and material nature awards us a body accordingly.

Question: How do you explain evolution?

Srila Bhaktipada: Evolution is the passage of the soul through the various species. It is not that the bodies of one species are changing into that of another; rather, it is the soul that is transmigrating. All 8,400,000 species are produced simultaneously by the Lord. In the human form of life, the consciousness is sufficiently developed so that the living entity can understand God and his relationship to God. Therefore we say that the real purpose of human life is to surrender to God in loving devotion. Otherwise, man is no different from the animals. The soul is there. The bodies are there. But the human being has a chance to put an end to transmigration by understanding God and surrendering to Him.

Question: The Bible speaks of man having dominion over

the animals. Just what is the position of animals in the creation?
Srila Bhaktipada: Some of the living entities are in superior
bodies, some in inferior. Generally, we consider the animal
species as inferior, but every living entity is an offspring of
the Lord. Krishna explicitly says, "It should be understood
that all species of life are made possible by birth in this material nature, and that I am the seed-giving father." (Bg. 14.4)
Although in a family there are intelligent children and unintelligent children, or beautiful children and ugly children,
the father loves all of them and sees to the welfare of all. He
may entrust his less intelligent children to the more intelligent,
but does this mean the intelligent children can kill and eat
the others? No. They are expected to protect the less advanced.

"Dominion" does not mean killing and eating; it means
protection. A king has dominion over all of his subjects, but
can he murder them at will? Because man's consciousness is
developed, he is expected to see to the welfare of all other
living entities. Nowhere in the Bible is it stated that only
man has a soul. I challenge you to find such a passage. But
it teaches that God is the Father of everyone. "And God made
the beast of the earth after his kind, and cattle after their
kind, and every thing that creepeth upon the earth after his
kind; and God saw that it was good." (Gen 1.25) Where does
it say, "God made the beast of the earth, but He gave it no
soul," or, "God made the beast of the earth for man to slaughter"?

Because God has consciousness, the living beings also have
consciousness. Because man has dominion over animals, he
must see to their welfare. And what is welfare? Due to their
previous karma, they are placed in their particular bodies to
fill out their term, just as a prisoner is sentenced to jail for
a designated period. This sentencing is both a kind of punishment and an opportunity to learn. That learning experience
should not be interrupted. When we kill an animal, we interrupt his term of life in that particular species. In other words,

his evolutionary progress is checked, and he has to return to that species again to fulfill his term. Instead of impeding his progress, we should help by giving him a little *prasadam*, food offered to the Lord with love and devotion. Then he can make rapid evolutionary progress. Or if the animal can just hear us chanting the names of God, he will benefit. It is said that when Lord Chaitanya chanted Hare Krishna in the Jarikanda forest, all living entities—animals, birds, trees, creepers—benefitted to the highest degree. And by the Lord's potency, the tigers and deer even embraced each other and chanted Hare Krishna. On another occasion, when a dog took some food from Lord Chaitanya's hand, the dog immediately became perfect in spiritual consciousness and went back to the Kingdom of God that very day.

Both human beings and animals engage in eating, sleeping, defending, and mating, but the human being is different in that he has the developed consciousness by which he can inquire, "Why am I here? Why am I suffering? I am going to have to die. What then? Is there life after death? Is there a Supreme Being?" An animal cannot ask these questions. Although they are suffering in degraded bodies, they do not know it. A hog wallowing in stool may see another hog slaughtered, but he does not think that this will happen to him. No. He's content wallowing in stool, thinking he's happy. Similarly, a man lying intoxicated in the gutter may think he's happy, but a sober man can see that his condition is miserable. Of course, in a larger sense, all material bodies are miserable. Therefore Krishna says, "From the highest planet in the material world down to the lowest, all are places of misery wherein repeated birth and death take place." (Bg. 8.16)

In many ways, an animal is like a small child. When we see a child behaving in an undesirable way, we think, "Oh, give him a few years. He'll grow up and act properly." In the same way, if an animal is left alone, his consciousness also develops after a few lifetimes. But in the meantime, as more advanced elder brothers, we should protect and help him along. This is what is meant by "dominion."

Question: Well, most people follow pretty contradictory policies toward animals. Cows and hogs are raised for slaughter, and to justify this, people say that they have no souls. Yet people protect dogs, give them names, pamper them like family members, and even give them Christian burials. What does this mean?

Srila Bhaktipada: It means that people have lost their intelligence. They are not really looking at the matter philosophically. They should ask, "Why do I like one animal and want to kill another? Why do I preserve this one and slaughter that one?" Obviously, the only motive is sense gratification. Because a dog is giving sense gratification in one form, they keep him as a pet. And because the cow gives sense gratification in the form of a steak, they kill it.

The end result of this attitude is: "Whatever gets in my way, let me kill it." This was Hitler's attitude toward the Jews. He said, "These people are not fit to live. Let us exterminate them." If we do not understand the nature of the soul and do not revere the soul as part and parcel of God, we will come to the point where we'll gladly slaughter our own children for sense gratification. It is stated in *Srimad-Bhagavatam* that at the end of this age of Kali, parents will raise children simply for food. Remember Jonathan Swift's "Modest Proposal"? He satirically proposed that children be raised for food. And today we are not far from this point, are we? Presently, mothers are murdering their children within the womb because they interfere with their sense gratification. If they will kill children in the womb, why not eat them also? In fact, we have already heard that a certain restaurant in New York is serving human fetuses as "delicacies."

Question: Didn't Srila Prabhupada connect animal slaughter with wars?

Srila Bhaktipada: Yes, he often said that as long as people kill and eat animals, there will be war. There's a direct connection between the slaughterhouse and the battlefield. Because people have no knowledge of the law of karma, they do not realize what they are doing to themselves. It is a fact that meat-eating makes people more aggressive. Also, according to the law of karma, when we slaughter an animal, we have to return in an animal body and be slaughtered in turn. And who slaughters the animal? The farmer who raises it, the truck driver who transports it, the butcher who kills it, the shopkeeper who sells it, the cook who prepares it, the waiter who serves it, and the person who eats it. All are involved. Any way you look at it, the future is bleak for a society that legalizes slaughter.

Question: What do you mean when you say that we determine our next body?

Srila Bhaktipada: This science is explained in *Bhagavad-gita.* Whatever we think of at the time of death, that state we attain. If we live like a dog or hog, we establish that pattern of thought, and, at death, nature gives us the body for which we've prepared ourselves. "Whatever state of being one remembers when he quits his body, that state he will attain without fail." (Bg. 8.6) Krishna is fulfilling everyone's desire.

The Vedic literatures tell of Maharaj Bharata, who renounced his kingdom and went to the forest to practice austerities for spiritual advancement. One day, he saved a fawn whose mother had drowned in a river. Being a compassionate soul, Maharaj Bharata took the deer back to his hermitage and raised it. Gradually he became so attached to the deer that he even neglected his spiritual practices. One day, while he was searching for the deer, he died, and because he was absorbed in thinking of the deer, he was forced to accept a deer's body in his next life. By the grace of God, however, he could remember his previous life and his desire for Krishna consciousness. Therefore, even though in a deer's body, he gave up the company of other deers and searched out the company of great sages in the forest. When he found them, he listened to their discussions about Krishna consciousness.

Thus, when he gave up the deer's body, he took his next birth as a great sage. The point is that we determine our next body by our thoughts and activities in this one. Nothing is haphazard or whimsical. Our next life is a natural continuation of this life.

CHAPTER EIGHT

The Problem Of Evil

Question: When we speak of evil, we refer to something that is morally bad, that causes pain or injury to oneself or others. This is a general definition found in any dictionary. How would evil be defined in the Vedas?

Srila Bhaktipada: According to *Isopanishad*, there is no evil in the absolute sense. *Om purnam adah purnam idam purnat purnam udacyate.* "The Personality of Godhead is perfect and complete, and because He is completely perfect, all emanations from Him, such as this phenomenal world, are perfectly equipped as complete wholes." (*Isopanishad*, Invocation) Evil is the illusion that arises when there is no consciousness of the all-perfect Absolute Truth, or God. As soon as we identify ourselves with these material bodies, we place ourselves in an evil or illusory state by thinking we are what we're not. We have forgotten our real identity as eternal servants of Krishna. For a follower of the Vedas, the only evil is forgetfulness of God, or ignorance of the Absolute Truth. In that forgetful state, we perceive God's perfect creation as imperfect or evil.

Question: Why did this forgetfulness come into the world?

Srila Bhaktipada: Since we come from God, we are eternally related to the Lord in a perfect loving relationship. But as soon as we forget God or want to imitate God, we are given a chance to fulfill our desires in the material universe. This entire material universe, located under a great cloud called the *Maha-tattva*, occupies only a small segment of the limitless spiritual sky. Here, due to our rebellious desires, we are given a chance to play like lords of creation. We are like children imitating their father. Since children do not have the ability to act like their father, they simply make disturbances. Therefore the father says, "Here are some toys. Now you can play and not cause any disturbance." Thus we play in this temporary material world, acting out our material desires, pretending that we are God.

But we can never become God. We are His eternal servants. Nor can we play like children forever. No. Old age, disease, and death come to remind us of our real position. Finally, after many, many births of bitter experience, when we realize that we are not controllers but controlled, then we surrender unto God, leave the unreal playground, and enter into the reality of the Kingdom of God by rendering transcendental loving devotional service.

Question: Why didn't God create a universe that is eternally situated in goodness?

Srila Bhaktipada: He did. It's called the spiritual sky, the Kingdom of God. There, goodness, or godliness, never declines, because no one ever forgets Him. In this material world of illusion, however, everything must wind down, like a clock. Here the quality of goodness is gradually dissipated due to God's covering feature. Of course, Krishna is the original source of all energy, but due to forgetfulness, we lose contact with Him. Thus the quality of goodness, coming from the all-good Supreme Person, gradually declines, and we become more and more forgetful.

In the golden age of Satya-yuga, the quality of goodness gradually decreases to 75%; in the Treta-yuga, goodness further declines to 50%; in Dwapara-yuga, still further to 25%; and as Kali-yuga advances, even that becomes lost. Presently we have passed through five thousand years of Kali-yuga, and some 428,000 years remain. So this process takes some time. Finally, at the end of Kali-yuga, the world is in such a chaotic condition—people reduced to the size of pigmies, eating their own children for food—that God comes on a white horse with sword in hand, as the Kalki avatar, not to preach, but to destroy the miscreants and reestablish the principles of goodness. Thus God winds up the clock, and another Satyayuga begins.

Question: Are birth, old age, disease, and death necessities within this material world?

Srila Bhaktipada: As soon as we say "material," we indicate something temporary, which means that old age, disease and death must be there. Therefore these evils are inherent in material existence. Because we are eternal fragments of God, we naturally yearn for our eternal position in the Kingdom of God. When we try to live happily here in this temporary situation, we become like a fish trying to live on dry land. The situation is completely frustrating and impossible. Therefore in this material world, we are always anxious, always in distress. It is an incompatible situation: we are eternal, and this world is temporal.

Question: There's been much debate over what's morally evil. For instance, one man considers sex good, another considers it evil. Who's to decide these difficult moral questions?

Srila Bhaktipada: Morality must be decided by the Father of morality, Lord Krishna. In the absolute sense, nothing is bad because everything is emanating from God. That is the platform of pure Krishna consciousness. But since this material world is a place of forgetfulness of God, it is a world of duality, of good and evil. Unfortunately, somehow or other we have fallen into this temporal situation, and are suffering the miseries of birth and death. Now it's our job to get out. God even comes to help us by giving us instructions, laws, or moral codes, whereby we can gradually extricate ourselves.

We cannot establish our own morality. "Real religious principles are enacted by the Supreme Personality of Godhead." (Bhag. 6.3.19) We have to follow the process of purification set down by the Lord. Morality is not something subjective. It cannot be inaugurated or legislated by men. It is absolute because it is God's law. If God says, "This is right, and this is wrong," we have to accept it. He's the supreme controller and supreme judge. If we want to be moral, we have to abide by His laws.

Question: Recently, a high school teacher complained that her students are interested only in drugs, sex, and rock and roll–in that order. Now, if your teenage son said, "Dad, you're old fashioned. There's no evil. Everything's good, everything's God," how would you answer him?

Srila Bhaktipada: Everything is God in the sense that everything has been created by God and rests on His energy, but this doesn't mean that we can use everything in the same way. Both a brick and a pot are made of clay, but their use is not interchangeable. Hemlock and wild carrot may look the same to an untrained eye, but one is healthful and the other poisonous. Sometimes people say that since Lord Shiva smokes marijuana, we can too. This argument is false because Lord Shiva is very powerful and can do many things that we cannot. Lord Shiva once drank an ocean of poison, but if we try to imitate him, we will die. A small quantity of poison can kill us. Intoxication is poisonous because it makes us forget God. When intoxicated, a person thinks, "Everything's all right. I'm great. Everything will go on like this forever." Similarly, illicit sex gives us the euphoric feeling that we've attained the goal of life. If we can just have more and more, we will be completely happy. Of course, this is not a fact. Such pleasures last only for an instant.

Sense gratification can never satisfy us; it only makes us forget the real problems of life: birth, old age, disease, and death. If we don't die young, we must grow old. In old age, sense gratification, which seemed like nectar in youth, becomes bitter and poisonous. "A decrepit old man cannot enjoy sensual pleasure, nor can he renounce it. He is like a toothless dog which is only able to lick a bone with his tongue." (*Hitopadesa*, 1.120)

Moreover, sense gratification makes us forget the solution to life's problems: remembrance of God through pure devotional service. By accepting God's codes of morality and engaging in His service, we can solve all our problems, here and hereafter.

Question: Sometimes atheists argue, "How can an all-good God allow an orphan to starve, or an innocent family to be massacred?" How do you answer this?

Srila Bhaktipada: John Stuart Mill used to argue this way, and many atheists before him. And recently someone even wrote a book questioning why bad things happen to good people. Such materialists conclude that either God is not all good, or not omnipotent. Mill argued that somehow, in the great conflict between good and evil, God just doesn't measure up, or He's temporarily overcome by evil. Of course, we reject such theories. By definition, God is all powerful. He is also the source of everything. This would mean that He is also the source of evil, but in God there is no evil. What appears evil to us is good in Him, because He is all good.

What we call evil—sufferings, mishaps, etc.—actually comes upon us due to misuse of our independence. Factually, no one in this material world is innocent; everyone is here due to misdeeds in previous lives. "Be sure your sin will find you out." (Numbers 32.23) In God's prison, there are no innocent prisoners. If we break God's laws, we suffer. It is not that God wants us to suffer. He warns us not to come here, and He gives us His laws so that we can transcend this suffering condition. Therefore suffering is due to our willful disobedience of God and misidentification with this material body. Evil and suffering take place only on that illusory material platform.

God has given us everything, including good instructions, but if we reject them, how can we be happy? How can we blame God? By accepting the illusory material existence, based on this body, we create our own suffering. If God allowed us to be happy in this situation, He would be encouraging evil, or illusion. Therefore the devotee sees God's mercy at work in misery and suffering, because by suffering we are forced to recognize the fact that we are not the controller and do not belong here. It is due to suffering that most of us surrender to God and come to Krishna consciousness, and that is good. Indeed, the great Queen Kunti prayed to be put in such distress again and again, because at those times she was able to see Krishna, and seeing Krishna means never to see birth and death again.

Sometimes, when a child is sick, the mother has to deny him solid foods. This so-called starving of the child is meant to cure him. Seeing this, an ignorant person might say, "Why is this mother so cruel to her child? Why doesn't she feed him properly? Here, let me give him some bread and potatoes." Such ignorant compassion can kill the child. Compassion must be based on knowledge. When we know the disease and the real cure, we can be compassionate, otherwise our so-called compassion will only compound the suffering.

Question: We speak of Satan as "the evil one." Is it possible for an external force to impel us to evil acts?

Srila Bhaktipada: Arjuna asks Lord Krishna this question: "By what is one impelled to sinful acts, even unwillingly, as if engaged by force?" And Lord Krishna replies, "It is lust only, Arjuna, which is born of contact with the material modes of passion and later transformed into wrath, and which is the all-devouring, sinful enemy of this world." (Bg. 3.36-37)

This lust causes us to commit sin by identifying with the material body and acting on the material platform. As long as we think, "I am this body," we will try to enjoy the bodily senses more and more, and commit sinful acts in the attempt. "Thus, a man's pure consciousness is covered by his eternal enemy in the form of lust, which is never satisfied and which burns like fire." (Bg. 3.39)

An evil man thinks only of his own personal sense gratification, or that of his extensions in the form of family, society, friends, or nation. At the beginning of *Bhagavad-gita*, Arjuna was thinking this way, but Lord Krishna enlightened him by telling him to think of God always and surrender unto Him.

In this way, the enemy lust can be controlled. Arjuna was
saved when he agreed to act according to Krishna's orders.
"My dear Krishna," Arjuna said at the conclusion of
Bhagavad-gita, "O infallible one, my illusion is now gone,
I have regained my memory by Your mercy, and I am now
firm and free from doubt and am prepared to act according
to Your instructions." (Bg. 18.74) Similarly, we will never
conquer evil or solve life's problems until we come to the
same conclusion and surrender to Krishna.

Question: According to Christianity, we are born into original
sin due to Adam's fall. But why did Adam sin? Ultimately,
wasn't God the cause?

Srila Bhaktipada: God is neither sinful nor evil. The origin
of sin is in the living entity's misuse of his minute independence. As I said before, without independence, we would be
robots. Machines cannot be sinful; a machine does just what
it is designed for. A computer functions according to its pro-
gram. God gives man the independence to decide: "Yes, I will.
No, I won't." Otherwise, love of God would be impossible. A
machine cannot love anyone. God has created us to
love Him by our own free choice. Why? Because He takes
pleasure in our loving and glorifying Him. And when He is
pleased, we are also pleased. Only when we misuse our independence is this loving exchange interrupted.

If we do not want a life of responsibility, perhaps we would
like to be animals. An animal is like a computer programmed
by material nature. Animals don't go on diets. They eat according to their nature. Cows eat grass, and tigers eat flesh. This
doesn't mean that tigers are less moral than cows. Because
animals are programmed by nature, they act instinctively.
There is no question of sin. But man can sin because he has
been given the ability to discern right from wrong and the
independence to choose between them. The greater the gifts,
the greater the responsbility.

Question: Catholicism distinguishes between mortal and ve-
nial sin. Mortal sins condemn a man to hell, whereas a small

sin can be atoned in purgatory. Do you agree?

Srila Bhaktipada: Yes. In *Srimad-Bhagavatam*, Sukadeva Goswami tells Maharaj Pariksit that one has to make atonement according to the gravity of the offense. The remedy for a cold is slight, but a severe illness may require surgery. In *Manu-samhita*, the original lawbook for mankind, we find various atonements. Some are slight and some are severe, depending on the offense.

Question: Christians often speak of Christ dying on the cross to redeem us from sin. Was such a sacrifice necessary?

Srila Bhaktipada: God does not have to kill His son to save us, but Jesus Christ was so compassionate that He willingly laid down His life to convince us of His love of God and to deliver us from the bondage of sin. "For this is my blood of the new testament, which is shed for many for the remission of sins." (Matt 26.28) God so loved us that He sent His son into the world to preach to us and set the example of a sinless life, and this makes us even more obligated to give up sinful activity.

We cannot use Christ as an excuse to sin. Sometimes people reason, "I can go on sinning. Christ will save me." This is the most heinous mentality. The spiritual master, or Jesus Christ, takes on the sins of his disciple because sin is like a great weight on one's shoulders; we cannot make progress and approach God with such a great burden. Therefore the Sanskrit word "guru" means "heavy." The guru says, "Give me your burden," but what can he do if we insist on collecting more burdens? St. Paul calls such activity "crucifying the Son of God afresh." (Heb 6.6)

Question: What then is the value of weekly confession?

Srila Bhaktipada: Confessing our sins is valuable if it helps us stop sinning. But our confession is useless if we think, "Oh, how convenient! I can say a few prayers, be absolved, and then go out and sin again." Is this not a mockery? "Be not deceived; God is not mocked." (Gal 6.7) God is the witness in our hearts. When we try to fool Him, we only fool ourselves.

We cannot continue sinning and make progress in spiritual life. Spiritual progress means becoming free from the bondage of sin.

Question: Is there such a thing as "the unpardonable sin"?

Srila Bhaktipada: No. God's mercy is so great that He can forgive anyone. "Though your sins be as scarlet, they shall be as white as snow." (Isaiah 1.18) Lord Chaitanya Mahaprabhu even saved the lowest debauchees, Jagai and Madhai. Lord Chaitanya was going to kill Jagai and Madhai because they had attacked His devotee, Lord Nityananda, but He forgave them because the devotees reminded Him, "Dear Lord, in this age everyone is sinful. Please show them Your mercy. If You don't, who will escape death?" Lord Chaitanya then forgave Jagai and Madhai, saying, "Give up your sinful activities and chant Hare Krishna. Otherwise you will surely face death."

We all face death. We all have to face the law of God. "The wages of sin is death; but the gift of God is eternal life." (Romans 6.23) Lord Chaitanya showed us that even the greatest sinner can be redeemed. Similarly, Christ forgave the adulteress: "He that is without sin among you, let him first cast a stone at her." (John 8.7) Then He told her, "Go, and sin no more." (John 8.11) In both cases, forgiveness was there, followed by the injunction, "Sin no more."

There is, however, one "unpardonable sin": blasphemy against God's holy names or against His pure devotee. In one sense, this sin cannot be forgiven because the sinner has severed the lifeline of forgiveness. "Thou shalt not take the name of the Lord thy God in vain; for the Lord will not hold him guiltless that taketh His name in vain." (Exodus 20.7) If we blaspheme the holy names, we reject the greatest mercy of God. What then, is left? The Lord has come personally in the sound of His holy names. And, out of mercy, He sends His pure devotee, or His perfect son, to save us. Can a drowning man be saved if he rejects the lifeline and fights off his rescuer? We are drowning because we so choose, but as soon

as we grab the lifeline of God's mercy by chanting His holy
name and surrendering to His pure devotee, we are saved.
There is no other way, but the door is open.

Question: Sometimes evil people seem to flourish, not suffer.
Do sins ever go unpunished?

Srila Bhaktipada: We may break the state laws and not be
caught, but there is no possibility of deceiving God. He is
present within the hearts of all living entities, witnessing their
activities. How long will a sinner flourish? For a lifetime? For
two or three lifetimes? Is there no justice, no future? "For I
the Lord thy God am a jealous God, visiting the iniquity of the
fathers upon the children unto the third and fourth generation
of them that hate me." (Exodus 20.5) No one can escape the
law of God.

The infamous atheist, Robert Ingersoll, used to make a
show of defying God at his lectures. He would stand at the
podium and say, "I don't believe in God. God does not exist.
If there's a God, let Him strike me dead within this minute!"
And he would take off his watch and count the seconds, and
at the end of a minute, he would say, "See! God doesn't exist!"

But why should God respond to such a fool? Of course,
now Ingersoll is dead, finally killed by God, who comes in
His own time for everyone. "I am death personified," Krishna
says (Bg.9.19). Just because a fool temporarily goes unpunished, we should not think that there's no punishment.
Rather, he's just being given enough rope to hang himself.
"The mills of God grind slowly, but they grind exceeding fine."

Nor does a devotee question why he is sometimes subjected
to suffering when he is trying his best to serve God. He understands that whatever he is suffering is due to his past sinful
activities. "I deserve to suffer more," he thinks, "but out of
mercy, God has mitigated my sufferings. If I just surrender
unto God, I can be with Him." Thus the devotee does not
worry about sinners escaping justice, or his own sufferings.
He spends his time following Paul's advice: "Speaking to your-
selves in psalms and hymns and spiritual songs, singing and

making melody in your heart to the Lord, giving thanks always for all things unto God." (Ephes 5.19) In this way, though he may suffer the inevitable pains of material existence, evil cannot touch him. He is happy because he knows that "all things work together for good to them that love God, to them who are the called according to His purpose." (Romans 8.28) Or, as Lord Krishna says, "Do not fear. I will give you all protection....Declare it boldly that My devotee never perishes." (Bg. 8.16, 9.31)

CHAPTER NINE

Heaven And Hell

Question: According to the Christian conception, Christ saves the faithful from hell. What is your view of this?

Srila Bhaktipada: Why not? A pure devotee can save someone from hell if he reunites him with God. First we have to understand what hell is. We create our own hell by choosing to separate ourselves from God. Hell exists both in the mind and also as a specific location. Milton wrote that "The mind is its own place, and in itself can make a heaven of hell, a hell of heaven." We can see that many people on this earth are carrying around their own private hells. Envy, lust, anger, and greed are demoniac qualities, and when a person comes under their sway, his life becomes hellish.

There is also a hell beyond this earth, and in the Vedas it is described as the lower planetary system. If one is impious in this life, he has to take birth on a lower planet, or in a lower species. In the lower planets, suffering is greater than on this earth because lust, anger, and greed are more prominent. Because the earth is located in the middle planetary system, we find both hellish and heavenly atmospheres here. Where there is God consciousness, the atmosphere is heavenly; and where there is a lack of God consciousness, it is hellish.

As soon as we are separated from God, we are factually in hell. God is the reservoir of all pleasure, and when we stray from Him, we are in hell. Lord Jesus Christ, or the spiritual master, comes to reunite us with God, to reestablish our God consciousness. The servant of God has no other business in the material world. He doesn't come here to enjoy sense gratification. Lord Krishna Himself spoke *Bhagavad-gita* to save us from suffering in a hellish condition. "Just surrender to Me, and I will deliver you from all sinful reactions," He said (Bg. 18.66).

Even though a devotee may be in a hellish place, he is in heaven because he is serving the Lord. Prahlad Maharaj specifically said that he was not concerned for his own position, whether in heaven or hell, because he could always think of Krishna and therefore always be happy. His concern was for the fools and rascals who were making elaborate plans for material happiness. No matter who they are, or where they are, such materialists create hell. But as soon as we remember the Lord, our mind is situated in heaven. The Kingdom of God is where God is King, and because a devotee is surrendered to the Lord, he is always in the Vaikuntha atmosphere, God's abode. Similarly, because a demoniac person is always envious of God and opposed to God, he is always in hell, regardless of his location. But although these atmospheres can exist anywhere, there are also specific places—heavenly planets and hellish planets. These are elaborately described in the Fifth Canto of *Srimad-Bhagavatam.*

Question: According to Catholic theology also, the greatest grief of those damned to hell results from being separated from God and realizing that they have lost God's association out of their own foolish pride.

Srila Bhaktipada: This reminds me of the teachings of Lord Kapiladev in *Srimad-Bhagavatam.* According to Lord Kapila, the living entity remembers his last one hundred lives while in the womb. In his miserable condition, cramped up tightly in the dark womb, the living entity remembers the mistakes he made: his sins, his neglect of God, his leaving God's Kingdom, and his forgetfulness of God. Then, in his misery, he calls out, "My dear Lord, just get me out of this terrible situation, and I will surely become Your devotee."

Unfortunately, when the living entity is born, he forgets this promise. "Our birth is but a sleep and a forgetting," says Wordsworth. Birth itself is painful and traumatic, and afterwards the child becomes conditioned to material life and identifies with the material body. Again his old habits and desires for sense gratification manifest. Still, by the evolutionary process, knowledge comes, and one eventually remembers, "Yes, I wanted to become God's devotee in this life. Let me give this life to God. Let me at last surrender to Him, and live for His pleasure only." The sooner we come to this realization, the quicker we get out of our hellish condition—material existence, or existence separate from God.

Question: What is the purpose of hell, or the hellish planets? What are the scriptural references?

Srila Bhaktipada: While it is true that in the Old Testament the conception of life after death is quite vague, there are a number of references to Sheol, which seems to be something like a big tomb where the dead lie inert. It is largely from the New Testament that we get our ideas of a place of reward and suffering where departed souls are subjected to the reactions of sins incurred during their lifetime. Perhaps the most famous reference is made by Christ Himself: "Then shall he [Christ the King] say unto them on the left hand, Depart from me, ye cursed, into everlasting fire, prepared for the devil and his angels...and these shall go away into everlasting punishment, but the righteous into life eternal." (Matt. 25.41,46) This clearly states that there is a judgement, and a condition following judgement wherein one suffers or enjoys according to his previous activities.

Question: Is such a judgement mentioned in the Vedic literatures?

Srila Bhaktipada: Yes, there are more than one. For instance, at the end of the four *yugas*, which make up one universal cycle, the Kalki avatar comes in judgement. During the cosmic manifestation, there are ten primary incarnations of Krishna. The first nine preach Krishna consciousness, and the last, Kalki, comes to destroy. Now we are in the last *yuga*, called the Kali-yuga. When this *yuga* ends in 428,000 years, Kalki will come, riding a white horse and carrying a sword. He will destroy all the miscreants and reestablish the golden age. There is a very similar description in the Book of Revelations. So the scriptures agree on this point.

That is one kind of judgement. There is another judgement, however, when each individual is judged at death. "It is appointed unto men once to die, but after this the judgement." (Heb 9.27) According to the Vedas, everyone is judged according to his karma by Yamaraj, the Lord of Death. If his activities are good, he is elevated; if they are bad, he is degraded.

Question: Christ spoke of everlasting punishment for sinners. Is this also confirmed in the Vedas?

Srila Bhaktipada: Just try to understand the difference between matter and spirit. Matter is measured by time and space. It composes a world of relativity, of duality. The spiritual world, however, is eternal, and its qualities are absolute. When one is condemned to the material world, it may seem like an eternity, but that is not possible. Matter is temporary. For an elevated living entity in the spiritual world, however, forgetting Krishna for one instant may seem like an eternity. Lord Chaitanya says, "O Govinda! Feeling Your separation, I am considering a moment to be like twelve years or more. Tears are flowing from my eyes like torrents of rain, and I am feeling all vacant in the world in Your absence." (*Sikshastaka*, 7) Even in this material world we see that intense pain seems to last forever. If we put our hand in a fire for one minute, that minute will seem like an eternity. Time is relative, not absolute.

God does not condemn someone eternally, with no further chance for rectification. What would be the point? Punishment is meant for correction. If there is no possibility of rectification, what is the purpose of punishment? Prisons, for instance, are meant to correct the criminal, who is condemned to suffer a certain sentence. Implicit in the punishment is the hope that afterwards the person won't commit any more crimes. Similarly, for the purpose of purification, God permits the living beings to suffer for a certain period according to their karma, or sinful activity. It is not that God wants us to suffer for the sake of suffering. He is not sadistic. How can we think that God can be so devoid of mercy that He would send His child to hell forever? As human beings, we have the qualities of God, if only to a minute degree. If mercy exists in finite creatures, it exists infinitely in God.

If someone goes to hell, he is not being punished needlessly. God always acts for the welfare of the living entity. He doesn't hate anyone; He loves everyone. It is the sin, not the sinner, that is hated because it separates us from God. We are all sons of God. How can the father wish to harm his son? He may punish him when he is naughty, but that is for his ultimate benefit. When the desire for rectification comes, the hellish condition passes.

We might consider the story of the prodigal son. When the errant son returned, his father ran to greet him, embraced him and affectionately welcomed him back. God is anxious to get us back, and His mercy is unending. But we have to learn to take advantage of that mercy by giving up our sinful habits. There is no other way.

Question: If God loves us, why doesn't He just let us all go to heaven?

Srila Bhaktipada: Krishna fulfills our desire. If we want to go back home, back to Godhead, we can, and He shows us the path. And if we want to remain apart from Him in the material world, and try to enjoy independently, we can. He will show us that path also. God doesn't interfere with our minute independence, but He wants us to return to Him. God is "not willing that any should perish, but that all should come to repentance." (2 Pet 3.9) If God loves us so much that He sends His son to die for us, He is certainly not going to make it impossible for us to surrender to Him at any point. But as long as we rebel against Him, we cannot enter the Kingdom of God, because that is a place of perfect harmony, of loving reciprocation with God. There is no envy there. If those who don't want to surrender to God are allowed there, how could there be peace? There would be strife, as in the material world, where nondevotees are always causing trouble for devotees.

God loves all of His sons. He doesn't hate anyone. Krishna says, "I envy no one, nor am I partial to anyone. I am equal to all. But whoever renders service unto Me in devotion is a friend, is in Me, and I am also a friend to him." (Bg. 9.29) If we want to become God's friend, He will be our friend. And if we want to be His enemy, He will be our enemy. Because Kamsa wanted to kill Krishna, Krishna became his enemy and killed him. Essentially, rebelling against God is the cause of death. Due to that rebellion, we are put into this material world and subjected to the cycle of birth and death.

What is that supreme, undefeatable power of death? Krishna says, "I am death personified." (Bg. 9.19). God is life, and God is death. For the devotee, death comes as Krishna, but for the nondevotee, Krishna comes as death. That force of death, which no one can resist, is God. But we can choose how we meet Him, and which of His faces we see. Even then, even if we miss that chance in this lifetime, God immediately gives us another chance to surrender to Him by placing us in another womb. As long as we fail to surrender, rebirth is there. That is Krishna's mercy for the nondevotee.

Question: Many people doubt hell's existence because they can't believe that an all-merciful, all-loving God would allow eternal suffering.

Srila Bhaktipada: That's a good point. Confusion arises because we use material terminology to describe spiritual phenomena. Since the spiritual world is absolute, the quality of punishment is eternal, but its duration is not. Because God is all loving, His justice is always tempered by love. "The quality of mercy is not strained." God's love is infinite, and we can never lose His mercy. As soon as we repent and turn from our rebellious activity, He is there waiting for us. We are all prodigal sons: as soon as we give up our life of false independence and riotous living, and turn back home, our eternal Father comes running to embrace us.

Question: Why, then, does Christ speak of "everlasting punishment," or Lord Krishna speak of "never approaching Me"?

Srila Bhaktipada: Because that's the actual quality. I remember once, as a small child, when I went blackberry picking with my parents, I wandered off into the woods and got lost. It was horrible. It was an eternity of loneliness. It seemed that I had been forever lost. It was indeed hellish. But when I found my way out of the woods, I was surprised to learn that I had been lost only about ten minutes. Hell appears eternal, but factually it too is material and therefore temporary. It is like a dream. In a dream, something may seem to go on and on forever, but in a second, when we wake up, the whole dream is ended. God is always there, waiting for us to turn our attention toward Him again. As soon as we surrender to Him, our hellish existence ends, just as a bad dream ends.

Question: In *Bhagavad-gita*, Lord Krishna speaks of lust, anger, and greed as being the three gates to hell. There must also be gates to heaven. What are they?

Srila Bhaktipada: There is only one—love, pure unalloyed love of God. Such love must be manifested, however, in many practical acts of devotion. It is also understood by four transcendental qualities: truthfulness, mercy, austerity, and purity.

Truthfulness refers to the Supreme Absolute Truth, God Himself. When we are situated in truthfulness, we understand that God is the cause of all causes and that we are His eternal servants. As long as we think, "I am this body," and act on the bodily platform, we are not established in truthfulness.

Mercy means distributing knowledge of God to others. We may give people material aid by feeding, clothing, and healing them, but because such mercy is on the bodily platform, it is temporary. Real mercy means showing a person the way home,

back to Godhead, and refraining from activities that impede
spiritual progress. Slaughtering animals, for instance, is a
cruel act that reveals insensitivity to the suffering of others
and therefore lack of mercy and compassion. We are all involved in the evolutionary process, and when we kill an animal, we deny him the chance to progress. Compassion must
be shown to all living entities by helping them in the progres-
sive march, according to their particular situation.

Austerity means to accept a simple life voluntarily in order
to maximize our service to God. We should use our valuable
time and resources to serve God. If we waste our time and
energy on sense gratification, that chance for service is forever
lost. Proper utilization of everything is an austerity, but it
brings peace and contentment.

Purity means cleanliness both within and without. Once we
take up the process of chanting the holy names of God, we
purify our consciousness. Then all these other qualities automatically develop in our heart and life. God is the supreme
pure and the supreme purifier. By associating with Him
through His holy names, we also become pure. The sun is so
pure that it can even purify stool and urine. How much more
powerful is the purifying potency of God's holy names! Therefore it is said that the holy names are the only way to salvation
in this age of Kali. They awaken our innate love for God and
thus open wide the gates to God's abode.

Question: How is heaven described in the Vedic literatures?

Srila Bhaktipada: Well, first we should understand that a distinction is made between the heavenly planets and Vaikuntha,
the spiritual sky, or the Kingdom of God. Generally, when
people think of heaven, they think in terms of sense gratification. If the senses are gratified, they think, "Oh, I'm in
heaven." And when the senses are deprived, they think, "Oh,
I'm in hell."

By executing pious activity, the living entity may be promoted to the heavenly planets, like Indraloka or Brahmaloka,
where the demigods drink soma and enjoy heavenly pleasures

for lifetimes lasting many thousands of years. But this is discouraged by Lord Krishna: "Men of small knowledge are very much attached to the flowery words of the Vedas, which recommend various fruitive activities for elevation to heavenly planets, resultant good birth, power, and so forth. Being desirous of sense gratification and opulent life, they say that there is nothing more than this....Men of small intelligence worship the demigods, and their fruits are limited and temporary. Those who worship the demigods go to the planets of the demigods, but My devotees ultimately reach My supreme planet." (Bg. 2.42–43, 7.23)

After living for thousands of years in the heavenly planets, the living entity must return to earth when the results of his pious activities are exhausted. Like hell, these heavens are not eternal. Only the transcendental abode of the Supreme Lord is eternal.

In *Bhagavad-gita*, Krishna describes that eternal Kingdom, the spiritual sky: "That abode of Mine is not illumined by the sun or moon, nor by electricity. One who reaches it never returns to this material world." (Bg. 15.6) Similarly, it is written in the Book of Revelations: "And there shall be no night there: and they need no candle, neither light of the sun; for the Lord God giveth them light: and they shall reign for ever and ever." (Rev 22.5) Again, Lord Krishna says, "There is another nature, which is eternal and is transcendental to this manifested and unmanifested matter. It is supreme and is never annihilated. When all in this world is annihilated, that part remains as it is. That supreme abode is called unmanifested and infallible, and it is the supreme destination. When one goes there, he never comes back. That is My supreme abode." (Bg. 8.20–21)

Ultimately, this is the meaning of the Kingdom of God: everything there is of the quality of God—*sat-chit-ananda*, eternal, full of knowledge and bliss. Like God, we, His parts and parcels, have eternal spiritual bodies that are innately filled with knowledge and bliss. At the present moment, however, this spiritual nature is covered by the gross material energy. Therefore we imagine ourselves to be American, Russian, Indian, male, female, human, animal, this, that. But how long will this illusion last? How long will we avoid asking the really significant questions? What is our eternal condition? What was our state before we took up these bodies? Only when we come to our original pure consciousness, Krishna consciousness, and reestablish our relationship with God as His eternal loving servant, can we return to the Kingdom of God.

Question: Then at one time everyone was an inhabitant of that spiritual sky?

Srila Bhaktipada: Yes. We have all come from God, who is eternally perfect. The individual spirit soul, being part and parcel of God, is also eternally perfect. We should not think that the soul is ever imperfect. The soul is perfect, but he is now covered, or illusioned. When we put on rose colored glasses, everything appears rosy. Similarly, because we are now seeing through this body, we are seeing things in a perverted way, as imperfect. Mistaking ourselves to be these bodies, we suffer birth, old age, disease, and death. We just have to understand our real eternal position. This has nothing to do with being Christian, Hindu, or Muslim. We have to understand the science of the soul, of self identity, which is the science of God consciousness. The sooner we realize that we have nothing to do with this material world, the sooner we can return to the Kingdom of God. This is done only by surrendering to God through the chanting of His holy name.

Question: Will everyone eventually return to God's abode?

Srila Bhaktipada: God will not force us to come back, but because love of God is a natural consequence of knowledge, we can expect that everyone will. In time, everyone will learn, either by careful hearing or hard-knock experience. An intelligent person can learn by hearing. If I say, "Don't jump off the roof. You'll hurt yourself," an intelligent person will take my word for it and save himself a lot of trouble. But a fool goes ahead and jumps to learn the same thing. To the saying "Experience is the best teacher" should be added "because a fool learns by no other." The Bible says that, for an intelligent man, faith comes by hearing. Hearing is all important. We have to hear the transcendental message of God and the vibration of God's holy name. If we hear over and over, our spiritual consciousness is aroused. We do not have to go to hell and experience suffering in order to learn. We can avoid all that by careful hearing from God or His representative, the bona fide spiritual master.

CHAPTER TEN

The Resurrection Of The Body

Question: Perhaps you could tell us something of the resurrection of the body in terms of Krishna consciousness. First of all, what is the Vedic analysis of the material body itself?

Srila Bhaktipada: It is a temporary creation composed of eight material elements: earth, water, fire, air, ether, mind, intelligence, and false ego. Although mind, intelligence, and false ego are subtle, they are considered material elements. Together, these eight elements compose the gross and subtle material body. Above all these is the real self, the eternal spirit soul. This temporary material body is like a covering for the soul.

Question: What are some of the soul's qualities?

Srila Bhaktipada: These are very beautifully described by Lord Krishna in the Second Chapter of *Bhagavad-gita:* "For the soul there is never birth nor death. Nor, having once been, does he ever cease to be. He is unborn, eternal, ever-existing, undying, and primeval. He is not slain when the body is slain....The soul can never be cut into pieces by any weapon, nor can he be burned by fire, nor moistened by water, nor withered by the wind. This individual soul is unbreakable and insoluble, and can be neither burned nor dried. He is everlasting, all-pervading, unchangeable, immovable, and eternally the same." (Bg. 2.20,23-24) No material condition can affect the soul, for he is *sat-chit-ananda*–eternal, full of knowledge and bliss.

Question: Christian doctrine holds that the souls of all men—both good and bad—will be reunited with their gross bodies

96

at the Second Coming of Christ. Could you clarify this?
Srila Bhaktipada: Did Christ say this? I don't think you can find such a statement in the Bible. I challenge anyone to show me the passage where Christ said such a thing. Rather, Christ said, "The hour is coming in which all that are in the graves shall hear His voice [the voice of Christ at the Second Coming], and shall come forth; they that have done good, unto the resurrection of life; and they that have done evil unto the resurrection of damnation." (John 5.28-29) This is not to say that the gross material body will be resurrected. Who would want to resurrect the same corruptible body? Hasn't this body caused us enough pain? The body is born, it grows old, suffers disease, and then dies. Why should anyone want to resurrect it? Such a doctrine, arising from misidentification and material attachment, perverts Christ's teaching.

The real purport here, which agrees with the Vedic teachings, is that this material body is but a temporary reflection of the spiritual body, which is *sat-chit-ananda*—eternal, full of knowledge and bliss. Because we have forgotten our real spiritual existence, we are identifying with gross matter. Gross matter, which is God's separated energy, undergoes six basic transformations: it comes into being, grows, stays for a while, produces some by-products, dwindles, and vanishes. Now, these changes are inherent in all material bodies. What sane man would want to undergo this process over and over? Such resurrection would appear to be just another name for reincarnation, or transmigration.

Instead of being concerned with resurrecting this gross body, we should try to attain our eternal spiritual body and go back to the Kingdom of God, where everything partakes of the superior spiritual energy, the internal potency of the Lord, being of the same quality as the Lord. That spiritual body is incorruptible. Here, everything is a perverted reflection of that spiritual existence, and therefore temporary. Instead of being eternal, and full of knowledge and bliss, the material body is temporary, and full of ignorance, misery, and anxiety. Its resurrection is certainly a ghoulish proposal.

Question: Some Christians are opposed to cremation because they feel that this body should be reasonably intact for the resurrection and Last Judgement. How would you answer this?

Srila Bhaktipada: I suppose they think it would be difficult for God to put the bodies back together if they're scattered here and there. Such a conception is certainly ridiculous. Being the supreme power, God can do anything. Suppose a man dies at sea. His body is cast overboard, fish eat the body, and people eat the fish. His body may then become part of hundreds or thousands of bodies. Then how is it resurrected? In what form? Who is being resurrected? This is ridiculous because it is based on misidentification of the real person, the soul, with the material body.

The material body is simply a lump of chemicals. Only when the soul comes in contact with it, is there life, movement, speech, thinking, loving, and so on. All these exist because the soul is present. It is not that the soul has somehow or other generated out of matter. This kind of theory leads to atheism. Modern scientists, for instance, are under the illusion that life, or consciousness, is generated from matter. That was also Dr. Frankenstein's theory, wasn't it? By piecing together all the parts of the body, he would create a man or a monster. For such scientists, matter is the basis of life. According to them, when matter develops to a certain stage, consciousness arises. Such a theory denies the existence of the eternal soul. But where is the evidence? Let them show us just one example of matter developing into a living force. Life comes from life. That is our practical everyday experience.

Furthermore, Krishna says that the spirit soul is the source of everything. Because of the soul's presence, material nature is activated. "As the sun alone illuminates all this universe, so does the living entity, one within the body, illuminate the entire body by consciousness." (Bg. 13.34) Without the soul, matter is lifeless. "Besides this inferior nature [earth, water, fire, air, etc.], there is a superior energy of Mine," Krishna says, "which is all living entities who are struggling with material nature and sustaining the universe." (Bg. 7.5)

If we plant a lemon seed, a tree grows, and that tree produces many lemons containing citric acid. But if we analyze the soil, we will not find any citric acid. How is this? The living entity within the tree is creating it. In all cases, matter is created due to the soul's presence. The universe is replete with examples of chemicals produced by living beings, but in no instance will we find consciousness being produced from matter. Since consciousness is the symptom of the soul, we can conclude that the soul produces matter, but matter can never create a soul.

Question: Would you explain, in Vedic terms, what happens at the moment of death?

Srila Bhaktipada: As long as we are not liberated, death means changing bodies. We are chained to these bodies due to our desire to enjoy sense gratification. We've come into this material world to enjoy material nature, and as long as this desire is there, we have to take one body after another. Bodies are awarded by nature according to our different desires. If we desire unlimited sex, we may be awarded the body of a pigeon, which has facilities for prolific sex. If we desire to eat voraciously, we may be given the body of an elephant. Nature affords different facilities according to our desires. If we have no material desires, if we want only to serve and love God, we will not be given another material body but will attain a spiritual body to fulfill our spiritual desires in the Kingdom of God. Lord Krishna says, "And whoever, at the time of death, quits his body, remembering Me alone, at once attains My nature. Of this there is no doubt." (Bg. 8.5)

It is therefore most important to develop our dormant love of Krishna and our desire to serve Him and think of Him always. Sense gratification is available to all living entities. Why waste our human life trying for what any dog or hog can enjoy? Sense gratification is there in every species of life. Human life is meant for developing a higher consciousness by which we can understand ourselves to be eternal. By rendering service to God, we understand ourselves to be part and parcel of Him, and by loving God, we develop the desire to return to Him. Thus always thinking of God, we will go to the Kingdom of God at the time of death, and live with Him eternally in a spiritual body.

Question: In the Vedic literatures, is there such a thing as the Last Judgement, or Second Coming?

Srila Bhaktipada: Before understanding Christ's second coming, we have to understand His first. The descent of Christ two thousand years ago was God's coming into the world for the purpose of preaching Krishna consciousness. That was not the first time God has come, nor will it be the last. "Whenever and wherever there is a decline in religious practice," Krishna says, "and a predominant rise of irreligion—at that time, I descend Myself." (Bg. 4.7)

Krishna either comes personally, or sends His son or representative, the bona fide spiritual master. One who descends into the material world from the spiritual world in order to preach God consciousness is called an *avatara*. The Lord will certainly come again. Whether we call it the second coming, or the third, fourth, or hundredth coming, God comes again and again. The Lord never abandons the fallen souls. It is not that He comes once, and, if we don't hear His voice, He forgets us. He can never forget us. He is our eternal Father. Do you think that if a father calls his son once, and his son doesn't respond, the father will abandon the son forever? The son may sometimes forget the father, but the father never forgets the son. Therefore in this age Krishna has so kindly incarnated in the form of His name. Hare Krishna is actually the incarnation of God in the form of sound. There is no difference between the Lord and His name.

The last judgement actually refers to the destination of the subtle material body. The Bible states that "it is appointed unto men once to die, but after this the judgement." (Heb 9.27) Death is there to judge whether or not we have developed our

Krishna consciousness in this life. Death is the final examination. If we think of the Lord, we pass. But if we have material desires—if we think of our family, country, society, or sense gratification of any kind—then nature affords us another body to fulfill our desires. The subtle material body composed of mind, intelligence, and false ego, is attracted to the womb of a particular type of mother, and then a new body is developed.

Question: In Christianity, there's belief in a risen, resurrected body without human defects, invested with the special qualities of God's own glorified body. Could you tell us something about the spiritual body, according to the Vedic conception?

Srila Bhaktipada: First of all, the words "God's glorified body" imply that at one time God's body wasn't glorious. God's body is the eternal form of Absolute Glory. It is eternal, full of knowledge and bliss. Christians may speak of these material bodies being glorified because at the present moment they are not glorious. But it is more accurate to understand that the material body is always subject to the fourfold miseries—birth, old age, disease, and death—and is therefore always an embarrassment for the eternal spirit soul. Under illusion we are thinking, "I am this body, but someday this body will be glorified." But in truth, we have nothing to do with these bodies.

As spirit soul, we are always unborn. Why identify with these bodies that are doomed to perish? "Dust thou art, and unto dust shalt thou return." (Gen 3.19) As soon as the soul departs, the body returns to dust. It is not the soul that becomes dust. We have to get rid of this confusion resulting from misidentification.

Inability to understand the transmigration of the soul from one body to another is due to excessive attachment for the material body, and this is the root cause of material bondage. Due to excessive attachment to body and family, people are hoping, "Oh, in the afterlife, I will be reunited with my loved ones. I will see my wife again, my children again, and we will live happily ever after in heaven." But we have had hundreds and thousands of husbands, wives, children, and grandchildren. With which will we be reunited in heaven? Sometimes a person has to be reborn in his enemy's family due to negative attachment. To which family, then, will we go in heaven? This absurdity results from trying to take our material conceptions into the Kingdom of God.

Eternal life is there, but we must not think of it materially. We do have spiritual bodies, and these spiritual bodies have form. This material body covers the spiritual body, just as a glove covers a hand. Why does a glove have five fingers? Because the hand has five fingers. Similarly, this material body has form because the soul has form; it has senses because the soul has senses. On earth, spiritual realities exist pervertedly through the temporary material body and its relations, but in the Kingdom of God, they exist in perfection in relationship with the Supreme Personality of Godhead, Lord Sri Krishna. It is a mistake to think that we can transfer the material into the spiritual realm. It is only when we abandon material life that spiritual life manifests.

Question: Where is the eternal spiritual body when we are in these gross bodies?

Srila Bhaktipada: Where is the body you now have when you dream at night? In the dream, you may have the body of a king or that of a pauper. In the dream, the body you now have is forgotten, but this does not mean that it no longer exists. The dream body does not think, "Oh, this is my dream body. Where is my real body?" But still, the real body exists in another realm. Similarly, material existence is just like a great dream. Our spiritual body is outside the dream. When we wake up, we will find that it is right there where we left it. Therefore we chant Srila Bhaktivinode Thakur's prayer, *"Jiv jago, jiv jago!"* "Wake up! Wake up! Don't you know that you are sleeping on the lap of the Maya witch?"

This whole material existence is the creation of the Maya witch, the witch of illusion who tempts us to forget God. The way to wake up is to remember God. As soon as we engage in

God's service and chant His holy names, we awaken our spiritual body. In that body, we can enjoy eternal life in the Kingdom of God.

Question: At death, does the spiritual body leave the material body?

Srila Bhaktipada: The spiritual body has nothing to do with this body composed of gross material elements. Just try to understand. You are not this material body. You are spirit soul, and you have a spiritual body, but that spiritual body exists only in the spiritual world.

Question: When we realize our eternal spiritual bodies, do we encounter loved ones in the spiritual sky?

Srila Bhaktipada: That depends on your relationship here. If the relationship is based on pure devotional service to God, then it will continue to exist. If it is a bodily attachment, it is illusion and must perish. Usually, such questions arise from material attachment. Why keep grasping at shadows? When you wake up from a dream, do you care about the people you met in the dream? No. You go about your real business and forget the whole dream, don't you? In the spiritual world, everyone is present, but our relationships will be different. Now we have many temporary relationships with family and friends, but in the spiritual world, we are all related to the Supreme Personality of Godhead, Lord Krishna.

When Christ was asked a similar question, He replied, "In the resurrection they neither marry, nor are given in marriage, but are as the angels of God in heaven." (Matt 22.30) In the spiritual abode, all relationships are transcendental and for His satisfaction.

Question: What is the best way to work toward the resurrection, or awakening, of our real spiritual body?

Srila Bhaktipada: Chant Hare Krishna. By chanting the Lord's names, we immediately revive our original, spiritual consciousness. This human body is likened to a good boat for crossing over the ocean of birth and death, the sea of illusion. The bona fide spiritual master is the expert captain, and the scriptures provide us favorable breezes. By taking advantage of all these facilities, we can swiftly cross the ocean and reach the other side, the Kingdom of God. It's up to us. We may either stay here and continue our material existence in one body after another, or, by the grace of God, make a successful crossing and enter into His eternal kingdom. The great voyage is before us. Hare Krishna!

CHAPTER ELEVEN

Healing

Question: It's well known that Christ healed many people and encouraged his followers to do the same. How do you view such healing?

Srila Bhaktipada: As soon as we speak of healing, the obvious question is "From what?" If our natural condition is one of good health, what has caused the disease? If we take the disease to be a malfunctioning of the material body, then is there a connection between disease and sin, or disobedience to God's law? On the one hand, God gives us everything for good health and eternal life, but inherent in these bodies are the material miseries of old age, disease and death. This is due to disobedience to God's law and our subsequent fall into material existence. In the spiritual world, there is no disease, old age, suffering, or death. There, everyone obeys God perfectly. Due to disobedience only, we have fallen into the material world. Significantly, *Paradise Lost* begins:

> Of Man's first disobedience, and the fruit
> Of that forbidden tree whose mortal taste
> Brought death into the world, and all our woe,
> With loss of Eden.

Although we lost absolute freedom from disease when we left the spiritual world, we increase our suffering here in this relative world by further disobeying God's laws. If we eat improperly, not following the regulations of the scriptures, the body deteriorates prematurely. If we engage in illicit sex, we contract vile diseases and shorten our life. If we take intoxicants, we destroy our bodies. Real healing means curing the cause of disease, which is the desire to break God's laws. On one occasion, Christ said, "Rise, take up thy bed, and walk." (John 5.8) First, He healed the body. Then He said, "Behold thou art made whole: sin no more." (John 5.14) But on another occasion, Christ said, "Son, thy sins be forgiven thee." (Mark 2.5) First He healed the soul, and then He proved His ability to forgive sins and thus the cause of disease by adding, "Arise, and take up thy bed, and go thy way...." (Mark 2.11)

The real point is to cure one from the root cause of disease, which is the tendency to commit sin. After all, even if you make a blind man see, can you guarantee that he will not become blind again, or that he will not grow old and die? Can you give him really important vision, spiritual vision? What is the value of twenty-twenty vision if we don't have eyes to see the beautiful form of the Personality of Godhead? What's the value of ears to hear if we don't listen to His transcendental instructions? *Srimad-Bhagavatam* says, "One who has not listened to the messages about the prowess and marvelous acts of the Personality of Godhead and has not sung or chanted loudly the worthy songs about the Lord is to be considered to possess ears like that of a snake, and a tongue like that of a frog." (Bhag 2.3.20) Of what value is healing the material body if we do not stop the disease and thereby stop the repetition of birth and death?

Question: What is your opinion of the popular faith healers who appear on television today? Are they genuine healers or frauds?

Srila Bhaktipada: There is no doubt that faith can heal. On the other hand, a man is a fraud if he doesn't cure the real disease. Just healing a man's body doesn't really benefit him, for he will again commit sin and be forced to suffer. Christ said, "Your fathers did eat manna in the wilderness, and are dead....I am the bread of life: he that cometh to me shall never hunger; and he that believeth on me shall never thirst." (John 7.49, 35) Unless one delivers the whole message of God for the cure of the spiritual being, he's a fraud.

Question: Specifically, how does sin create disease in our bodies?

Srila Bhaktipada: The natural function of these bodies is to serve God. If a machine is not properly used, it breaks down. If we don't serve God, we are forced by nature's laws to serve illusion. It is an illusion to think that we are the material body. By serving this illusion, we become diseased. It is something like polishing a birdcage and letting the bird within die of hunger. We are not the body, mind, or senses. We are spirit soul. Unless we feed the soul, we are sure to be diseased. Consequently, materialists are always in anxiety. They are always worrying, "Oh, someone may kill me. Someone is going to rob me. Maybe I will get sick. What is my future?" Such anxiety actually produces disease, but by following the laws of God, by plain living and high thinking, we can be happy and free of disease. But in any case, this material body is doomed to die. "From the highest planet in the material world down to the lowest, all are places of misery wherein repeated birth and death take place." (Bg. 8.16) Therefore, healing is valuable only if it stops the cycle of repeated birth and death.

Question: Christ often used healing to instill faith in the spiritually unsophisticated. Although the body is a dress, isn't health necessary for spiritual realization?

Srila Bhaktipada: Not necessary, but helpful. If a man is very sick, he may have difficulty thinking of God. Therefore King Kulashekar prays: "My dear Lord, may I die immediately now that I'm healthy so that the swan of my mind may enter into the stem of Thy lotus feet." Of course, if a devotee is surrendered, God will always give him a chance to chant His holy names.

Question: How do members of the Krishna consciousness movement treat disease and infirmities?

Srila Bhaktipada: We are engaged in stopping the cause of disease: life in this material world. This material body itself is the abode of disease. Krishna consciousness goes to the root cause of disease: rebellion against God. Material existence is a consequence of this rebellion. Until we surrender to God and return to His Kingdom, we will not be completely free of this disease. Therefore we are practicing austerities to come to the basic realization: "I am not this body. What am I? Spirit soul, servant of Krishna." When we come to understand "I am not this body," we experience great relief. That is the beginning of spiritual life. When we realize "I am not matter but spirit," we become free from hankering and lamentation. On the bodily platform, we are always hankering for something, and lamenting when we lose it.

Question: The evangelist Luke is referred to by St. Paul as "the most dear physician." (Col. 4.14) Would you visit a doctor when sick, or would you say "It's mind over matter," as Christian Scientists do?

Srila Bhaktipada: Certainly, the mind is very important in curing disease. Any doctor will tell you that a patient's mental outlook often determines whether he recovers or not. On the other hand, we don't accept the viewpoint that disease is simply a mental aberration that will go away if we forget about it.

We treat the body just as we would treat a vehicle. When it's not working properly, we take it to a garage for a tuneup. This body is a machine that the devotee uses for God's service, and he gives it whatever attention is required, but not more. We may give a car a tuneup, fill it with gas, and change the oil, but we don't have to polish it all day. The body doesn't require the amount of pampering that most people give it. Indeed, much disease in America is caused simply by overeating. Certainly the body requires food, but in moderation. Plain living and high thinking is the best policy.

Furthermore, we should understand that all healing comes from God, whether we are treated by a certified doctor, faith healer, or quack. Without God's sanction, no one can be cured. In *Bhagavad-gita*, Krishna says, "I am the healing herb." (Bg. 9.16) Therefore we should put our faith and trust in Krishna, the real healer, and surrender to Him. Krishna consciousness is not partial to one system of healing over another. We are partial only to Krishna.

Question: Christ spoke of physicians metaphorically once when He was criticized by the scribes and Pharisees. Can you recall this incident and explain it?

Srila Bhaktipada: "They that are whole have no need of the physician, but they that are sick: I came not to call the righteous but sinners to repentance." (Mark 2.17) This is certainly true. A healthy man has no need of physicians. Unless a man is fallen, he does not have to hear the gospel of repentance. But factually, everyone in this material world is fallen. If we are not sinners, why are we here? If a man is not a criminal, why is he locked in prison? This material world is a kind of prison for those who have rebelled against God. Therefore we require the great physician who can heal the soul by reestablishing our loving relationship with God. Our sickness is due to forgetfulness of Krishna. By remembering, loving, and surrendering to Him, we can be released from this abnormal, diseased condition.

Question: What did Christ mean when he said, "Physician, heal thyself"?

Srila Bhaktipada: If a physician cannot heal himself, what is the power of his medicine? This is the test of authenticity. What is the use in someone preaching the word of God if he himself transgresses God's instructions? The bona fide spiritual master must be free from vice—lust, anger, and greed— and he must be completely surrendered to God. He must also strictly follow the previous spiritual master. He cannot manufacture his own religion; he must follow the disciplic succession. Eternal religion means loving and serving God, that's all. Christ acknowledged this as the first and most important commandment. The spiritual master must be free from material disease himself before he can help others. He must be full of love of God, not love of this world. Therefore Christ said, "Physician, heal thyself." (Luke 4.23)

Question: Some yogis say, "I am not this body," but when they have a toothache, they run to a doctor. Does this mean that they are not transcendentally situated?

Srila Bhaktipada: They may have an intellectual understanding that they are not the body, but because such yogis generally don't understand the personality of God, their realization is incomplete, and they cannot maintain it. To understand theoretically that "I am not this body" is not sufficient for crossing over the ocean of material existence. The repetition of birth and death can be overcome only by the grace of the Supreme Lord, and we acquire that grace when we surrender to Him. Through loving service to God, we realize our eternal relationship with God, and by the grace of God, we can overcome all material obstacles.

CHAPTER TWELVE

The Universal Church

Question: Could you define and discuss the meaning of the universal church for us?

Srila Bhaktipada: The real church of God is not an organization, nor is it anything material. It is a spiritual entity composed of those who believe in God and love Him. In the Bible, the church is called the bride. A bride is a loving partner who assists and serves, and, as such, the church's real function is to assist the Lord in His earthly mission of reclaiming all conditioned souls. Being the all-loving Father, God doesn't want anyone to perish or remain away from Him. He wants to take everyone back home, back to Godhead, to live eternally in His spiritual abode. In this world, the church's mission is to assist God by being His instrument for the reclaiming of souls. Unless we unite on this platform of service to God, there is no question of unification or universality.

Question: Although religions recognize God as Father of all, there has never existed a truly universal church. What would be the common basis that could include everyone?

Srila Bhaktipada: First of all, the church cannot be sectarian, nor its doctrine imaginary. As soon as we begin interpreting God's word this way or that, there must be division. You have your interpretation, and I have mine. First, we have to know what God wants, and that will be our center of agreement.

There are many different religious faiths in the world—Protestant, Catholic, Hindu, Muslim, Buddhist—and a person may even change from one to another. A Hindu may be converted to Catholicism, or a Catholic to Protestantism, or a Protestant to Buddhism, or a Buddhist to Hinduism, and so on. These religious faiths are changeable, but real or essential religion cannot be changed.

In Sanskrit, we call this essential religion *sanatan dharma*, the eternal nature of all things, which specifically indicates the inherent, changeless nature of the living entity: to render loving service to God. Just as the inherent nature of water is liquidity, or the nature of fire is heat and light, or the nature of sugar is sweetness, so the eternal nature of the living entity, of every individual soul, is to serve.

We can see that every living entity, even in this world, is rendering service in some way or other. A man serves his wife and family. The shopkeeper serves his customer. A soldier enters "the service," and the police are said "to protect and serve." A dog has to serve his master, and an employee has to serve his boss. Even the president has to serve his country well in order to be elected.

Service is the common denominator unifying all. Everyone renders service, and we have seen that many people who no longer have a family to serve will serve a dog or cat. And finally, everyone serves the senses of the material body. Service must be there. We cannot escape it. It is our inherent nature. At the present moment, unfortunately, this service is imperfect, because it is misdirected. The mission of a universal church is to redirect that serving tendency toward its proper object, the Supreme Lord.

In material consciousness, a person serves with some ulterior motive. This is a symptom of imperfect service. A person goes to work and serves his employer because at the end of the week he gets a paycheck. If there is no paycheck, no further service will be rendered. The work isn't done out of love for the work itself, but for its result—money. This kind of service cannot satisfy anyone. The employer thinks the worker isn't working hard enough, and the worker thinks he isn't paid enough. In the material world, no one is satisfied with his service. But if we direct our service to God, satisfaction is guaranteed, even if the service appears to be imperfectly performed.

Of course, God is *atma-rama*, self-satisfied. He doesn't

need anyone's service to be complete. He is complete in Himself. But God feels pleasure in our love, and He reciprocates by lovingly supplying all necessities to His devotee. Although God doesn't need food or money—He is the proprietor and enjoyer of everything—He accepts whatever is offered in love. "If one offers Me with love and devotion a leaf, a flower, fruit, or water, I will accept it." (Bg. 9.26)

The devotee, in turn, is always satisfied by serving God because that service itself is unlimitedly rewarding. Rendering service to Krishna is our actual nature. Our eternal identity is Krishna Das, eternal servant of God. Therefore, devotional service is the real basis of unification, the foundation of the universal church.

Question: What are some of the tenets of this *sanatan dharma* religion that would be acceptable to all faiths?

Srila Bhaktipada: The first is the understanding that God is the center of everything. He is the creator, maintainer, and destroyer of everything. He is the Father of every living entity, not only human beings but also animals, plants, trees, aquatics—everyone. This is the platform of universal brotherhood. If we want to understand how all living entities are brothers, we have to know the universal Father, the original cause of all causes.

God must also be recognized as the enjoyer of everything. In the material world, people compete in order to acquire the objects of enjoyment. Everyone seeks his own sense gratification, but because material resources are limited, there is competition, and then greed and emnity. That is the cause of all strife in the world. We can put an end to this only when we recognize that everything is meant for God's enjoyment. We too are meant to be objects of God's enjoyment. Therefore, God's service should be our enjoyment.

When we understand God's position as master, we simultaneously recognize our own as servant. That is the platform of real peace and unity. When we recognize that all living entities are servants of God, we can cooperate, because there is a common center. Just as all the parts of the body—hands, arms, legs, head, feet—cooperate to serve the whole body, we should join together for God's service and enjoyment. If we try to avoid His service, we will have so many problems, for it is our constitutional nature to love and serve Him.

Question: But some people would say that we have the right to enjoy our God-given freedoms, including the right to serve or not to serve. How can a universal church unite such divergent views?

Srila Bhaktipada: We have to recognize that in this material world, there are always at least two views on any subject. Because we have minute independence, we can choose to agree with God or disagree. Whether you call them devotees and nondevotees, theists and atheists, saints and demons, there are always two basic types of men: those who recognize God as the supreme controller of everything and surrender unto Him, and those who rebel and refuse to accept His rule. In *Bhagavad-gita*, these two types of men are clearly described by their qualities:

"Fearlessness, purification of one's existence, cultivation of spiritual knowledge, charity, self-control, performance of sacrifice, study of the Vedas, austerity and simplicity; nonviolence, truthfulness, freedom from anger; renunciation, tranquility, aversion to fault-finding, compassion, and freedom from covetousness; gentleness, modesty, and steady determination; vigor, forgiveness, fortitude, cleanliness, freedom from envy and the passion for honor—these transcendental qualities belong to godly men endowed with divine nature." (Bg. 16.1-3)

Then Lord Krishna describes the demoniac: "Arrogance, pride, anger, conceit, harshness, and ignorance—these qualities belong to those of demoniac nature. Those who are demoniac do not know what is to be done and what is not to be done. Neither cleanliness nor proper behavior nor truth is found in them. They say that this world is unreal, that there is no foundation, and that there is no God in control. It is produced of sex desire, and has no cause other than lust. Following such conclusions, the demoniac, who are lost to themselves and who have no intelligence, engage in unbeneficial, horrible works meant to destroy the world. The demoniac, taking shelter of insatiable lust, pride, and false prestige, and being thus illusioned, are always sworn to unclean work, attracted by the impermanent. They believe that to gratify the senses unto the end of life is the prime necessity of human civilization. Thus there is no end to their anxiety. Being bound by hundreds and thousands of desires, by lust and anger, they secure money by illegal means for sense gratification." (Bg. 16.4, 7-12)

It is the same two paths described by Christ: "Enter ye in at the strait gate: for wide is the gate, and broad is the way, that leadeth to destruction, and many there be which go in thereat: Because strait is the gate, and narrow is the way, which leadeth unto life, and few there be that find it. Beware of false prophets, which come to you in sheep's clothing, but inwardly they are ravening wolves. Ye shall know them by their fruits. Do men gather grapes of thorns, or figs of thistles? Even so every good tree bringeth forth good fruit; but a corrupt tree bringeth forth evil fruit. A good tree cannot bring forth evil fruit, neither can a corrupt tree bring forth good fruit. Every tree that bringeth not forth good fruit is hewn down, and cast into the fire. Wherefore by their fruits ye shall know them." (Matt 7.13-20)

So, we can choose either path: to surrender to the Lord, and become His servant, or to surrender to our senses and to our personal, selfish desires. That is our God-given freedom, our minute independence. If we are intelligent, we will follow the Lord's instructions and act on His behalf. Then we will benefit, for we will become eligible to go back to Godhead at the end of this life.

Question: In a real sense, doesn't the universal church already exist? God is the Father of all, and we are all serving—some of us positively, some negatively. How could you begin to organize a *sanatan-dharma* institution?

Srila Bhaktipada: We are not concerned with creating an institution but with cultivating the consciousness by which all men will cooperate for God's service. That is the important point. Our concern is with spreading the message of Godhead so that people can understand that they are not this material body but eternal servants of God. When men realize their own true nature, they will automatically cooperate for the service of God.

Such realization is the impetus for all spiritual activities. God and His service are the axis of the creation. When we realize our relationship to God and establish a loving relationship with Him, all the miseries of material existence vanish, and the wheel of birth and death stops turning.

Miseries are inflicted on the living entity to show him that he's out of joint, to inform him that he's not serving the whole. When the body becomes sick, we immediately know that some part of the body is out of order. Until we center our consciousness on serving God, we will be sick in mind and body, and life will be hellish. As soon as we center everything on God, or Krishna, the universal church will manifest.

Question: How can Krishna consciousness claim to be such a nonsectarian, universal church when the movement has its own books and spiritual masters, different from those of other religions?

Srila Bhaktipada: That two plus two equals four is a truth found in all math books. It is true because it is a fact, and a religion is nonsectarian when it is factual, not speculative. It is a fact that God is the Supreme Being, and all living entities are His servants. This is spiritual realism. This scientific philosophy makes the Krishna consciousness movement nonsectarian.

We do not propose that people worship a new god or some local deity. There is only one God, one Supreme Lord, regardless of what we call Him. God has thousands and millions of names. True, Moses and David may not have chanted the Hare

Krishna *maha-mantra*, but we don't claim that God is restricted to particular names. The real goal is God consciousness, surrender to God.

Question: If such a universal church ever came about, who would its leaders be? How would they qualify?

Srila Bhaktipada: Again you are thinking materially in terms of an institution. Such leaders wouldn't be elected. It is not a matter of political campaigning. You cannot create a man of God by rubber-stamping a title on someone. A man of God is known by his qualities. Either one is surrendered to God, or he isn't. Our best course is to concentrate on developing the qualities of a God-surrendered soul. Unless we develop those godly qualities mentioned in *Bhagavad-gita*, there is no question of leading others. These qualities automatically develop when we cultivate Krishna consciousness: always remembering the Lord, chanting His holy names, and engaging in His service twenty-four hours a day. When we become Krishna conscious, all our sinful thoughts and activities stop.

Question: What particular manifestation of the Personality of Godhead would be worshipped? Christians wouldn't abandon devotion to Christ any more than you would to Krishna, or Buddhists to Buddha.

Srila Bhaktipada: That is correct. And why should they? A person should not give up his particular mode of worship, or stop calling God by the name he's familiar with.

In this regard, the *Chaitanya-charitamrita* tells an interesting story about Rupa and Sanatan Goswami and their younger brother Anupama. Rupa and Sanatana, the great devotees of Lord Chaitanya, excavated and reestablished all the holy places in Vrindaban, the land where Lord Krishna appeared five thousand years ago. Like Lord Chaitanya, Rupa and Sanatan Goswami worshipped Krishna in ecstatic love and were situated in the most elevated position of devotional service. Their brother Anupama, however, was a great devotee of Lord Ramachandra from his early childhood. One day, after listening to much preaching and persuading, Anupama relented and agreed to become a Krishna *bhakta*. But that night, he began to think, "How can I give up the lotus feet of my dear Lord Ramachandra?" Anupama spent the whole night crying because of this. The next morning, he told his elder brothers, "I have sold my head at the lotus feet of Lord Ramachandra. I cannot take it away. That would be too painful for me." On hearing this, Rupa and Sanatan Goswami praised him, and when Lord Chaitanya heard of Anupama's loyalty, He exclaimed, "Glorious is that devotee who does not give up the shelter of his Lord, and glorious is that Lord who does not abandon His servant." (*Chaitanya-charitamrita*, Antya 4.35-46) It is not worship of a particular name or form of God that is important, but our love and faith.

Similarly, devotion to Christ and the chanting of His name need not be abandoned. Interestingly enough, the names Christ and Krishna are similar. The Greek word "Christos" means "to anoint," and the Sanskrit word "Krishna" means "all attractive." Now, who is the anointed? The all-attractive Supreme Personality of Godhead, who attracts everyone by His wealth, fame, beauty, strength, knowledge and renunciation. He is the anointed. Only God is fully qualified because only God possesses all these attractive qualities in full. The words Christ and Krishna are identical in meaning because they refer to God. Therefore it doesn't matter whether you chant "Christ" or "Krishna." "For whosoever shall call upon the name of the Lord shall be saved." (Romans 10.13)

That's the real point: chanting the name of God and taking shelter of Him. No other shelter will help us—not alcohol, not LSD, not our friends, family, or country, nor anything else of this material world. We have to call on God and God alone. *Harer nama harer nama harer namaiva kevalam kalau nasty eva nastya eva nasty eva gatir anyatha.* "In this age of Kali, there is no other religion than the glorification of the Lord by the chanting of His holy name. That is the injunction of all the revealed scriptures. There is no other way, no other way, no other way." (*Brihan-naradiya Purana*) By calling out to Him in helplessness, we become like a child calling to his parent, "Dear father! Dear mother! Please help me!" Immediately the parent comes to help the child. As soon as we sincerely call out to the Lord, He will pick us up from this material life and again situate us in His eternal service.

Question: The Old Testament says, "Thou shalt not make thee any graven image." (Deut 5.8) Aren't images, or idols, an important part of your temple worship? And couldn't this be called sectarian?

Srila Bhaktipada: If a human being, a conditioned soul, manufactures an idol of God, that is certainly a strange god or graven image. God cannot be manufactured by a finite creature. Therefore we condemn mental speculation. We cannot hope to figure out God by using our tiny brain power or artistic skill.

This, however, does not mean that God cannot reveal Himself to His pure devotee. If we accept the form of the Lord as revealed by the Lord Himself, that form cannot be considered manufactured. It is a form received directly from the Lord out of His causeless mercy.

No one can say that God cannot appear before man, or that God cannot appear in the form of wood, stone, jewels, or anything else. In the Shastras it is stated that God incarnates in forms of wood, stone, paint, jewel, or mind because these are all His own energy. Since everything comes from God, God can reveal Himself through anything, if He so desires. That initiative, however, comes from God, not from man. We cannot carve some statue and say, "I have created God." This would be properly called idolatry. Rather, we must worship in the way authorized by God.

The Krishna consciousness movement is not manufactured by any individual. It is not something that Srila Prabhupada or any other person has made up. No. It is the authorized process revealed in the Vedic literatures and handed down by the self-realized *acharyas*. No one should accept this or any other philosophy blindly. Therefore Srila Prabhupada has given us scores of books to enable us to understand everything with our minds as well as our hearts.

Question: Can the Communists—or any atheistic state, for that matter—be included in a universal church?

Srila Bhaktipada: No. How can they? The Bible prohibits us from uniting with such ungodly persons. "Wherefore come out from among them, and be ye separate, saith the Lord, and touch not the unclean thing; and I will receive you." (II Cor 6.17) The devotees of the Lord are different, and their activities yield different results. It is foolish to think that one can do just as he pleases and then in the next life get the same results as one who is devoted to God. That is a popular philosophy, however. Some people believe that at the end of life, everyone is dead and everything is zero. Others say that we all go to a happy land and get the same results. What nonsense! There is no evidence of this. Certainly not in our past experiences in this life. "Be not deceived; God is not mocked: for whatsoever a man soweth, that shall he also reap." (Gal. 6.7)

In *Bhagavad-gita*, Krishna says, "Those who worship the demigods will take birth among the demigods; those who worship ghosts and spirits will take birth among such beings; those who worship ancestors go to the ancestors; and those who worship Me will live with Me." (Bg. 9.25) According to our activities, we receive specific results. "For the wages of sin is death; but the gift of God is eternal life...." (Romans 6.23) If we choose to commit sinful activity, we will have to face both physical and spiritual death. And if we choose to surrender to God, we will enter into an eternal life of knowledge and bliss. That is the realm of the Kingdom of God. By rendering service to God in loving surrender, we can go back home, back to Godhead. That is the process recommended by all saintly teachers and scriptures.

Question: Years ago, linguists tried to establish an international language—Esperanto. It was an artificial attempt, and it failed to catch on. Now English is quickly becoming that international language by a natural process. Do you think that a universal church will naturally develop and catch on like that? Will it be a religion that everyone will automatically agree to?

Srila Bhaktipada: Yes, that is exactly correct. In *Srimad-Bhagavatam* it is stated that in this age, the religion that can be easily performed and that will be pleasing to all men will be the chanting of the holy names of God. "There is one special advantage about this age of Kali-yuga: people can attain liberation and return home, back to Godhead, simply by chanting the Hare Krishna *maha-mantra*." (Bhag. 12.3.51)

This method is easy and sublime. Kali-yuga is considered to be an ocean of faults, but this one great boon nullifies them all. Through the sound of His name, God has made Himself freely available to everyone. The foolish, the learned, the rich, and the poor can all chant the holy names of the Lord. God is so great that He has thousands and millions of names, and He is present in all of them. If we just take to chanting them sincerely, we will become God conscious, or Krishna conscious. Then the universal church will automatically manifest itself.

CHAPTER THIRTEEN

Conversations With Christians
(1)

(A conversation with Professor Harvey Cox of Harvard, Professor Lee Daugherty of the West Virginia College for Graduate Studies, and students)

Dr. Cox: I first met Kirtanananda Swami Bhaktipada in 1970, when I invited him and a group of devotees to come to Harvard Divinity School to do some chanting and make a presentation in the newly opened Rockefeller Hall. That was a memorable occasion. So we're very happy to be here with you this morning.

Srila Bhaktipada: I'm very happy you've been so kind as to come visit us here at New Vrindaban.

Student: I'd be interested to know how you felt about your reception in 1970 at Harvard, and in general how you see things as changing. Have you seen more receptiveness to the Hare Krishna movement from educated people?

Srila Bhaktipada: Among educated people, our reception has always been quite good. People who are familiar with the tradition of Lord Chaitanya, Vaishnavism, immediately understand that we are an authentic, bona fide movement. And in general, the further you get away from that position of knowledge, the more you find people susceptible to prejudice and suspicion. In this area of West Virginia, the neighbors who know us and have regular dealings with us all like us, but those who have never had any contact with us have the typical reaction of one who is ignorant: "Something strange has come into our environment." Certainly, if one understands the main principle of any religion, he immediately recognizes that same principle here. The main religious principle is love of God.

Student: Right. I don't think a lot of people see that.

Srila Bhaktipada: Because they don't recognize the religious principle in their own faith. We have to make a distinction between religious faith and religion. Buddhism, Christianity, Hinduism, Mohammedanism, and Judaism are all faiths. You can change your faith—you may be born a Christian and then decide to become a Jew—but you cannot change your religion. The Sanskrit word is dharma, and that refers to our inherent nature. The dharma of fire is to give off heat and light. You can't take that quality away. Our actual nature is that we are part and parcel of God. That cannot be changed. And to develop that relationship is the religious principle. One may be born a Christian, but if he actually understands this principle, he'll recognize it anywhere. If he doesn't, then he doesn't recognize it in his own religion. He is simply following rituals and dogma.

Dr. Daughtery: Would you be willing to share with us something of your own personal journey? I think you told us once before when I was here that you had been raised in a Christian tradition.

Srila Bhaktipada: Yes. My father was a Baptist minister.

Dr. Daughtery: How did you get from there to where you are now?

Srila Bhaktipada: Sometimes it's difficult to look back and see how you came. You just know that by the grace of Krishna, you came. As a child I was always very much absorbed in God consciousness. I used to gather my playmates together and preach to them. When you're a child, people are always asking what you want to be when you grow up. I wanted to be a missionary. And I guess I am a missionary.

Dr. Cox: Still getting your friends together and preaching. Well, here we are.

Srila Bhaktipada: As a teenager, I went through a period of doubt and disillusionment and agnosticism. But that was not satisfying. In graduate school, when I was working on my doctorate in American history, I still couldn't get away from the religious aspect. For my dissertation topic I chose "Religious Revivalism in the Old South." So religion was still there, but I was approaching it from the academic point of view, which is like trying to know the taste of honey by licking the outside of the bottle. In the end, I decided that rather than simply record religious history, I would participate in it.

Religion is not a spectator sport. It's something you get involved in. Because it is based on faith, there's no question of understanding it from the outside. Of course, our faith should not be blind. It should be rational and reasonable. I have faith that you have a father and mother, although I've not met them. That's certainly not unreasonable. Similarly, to understand God as the cause of all causes is not unreasonable. We can see that everything has its cause; therefore there must be an original cause. *Govindam adi-purusam tam aham bhajami.* Govinda, Krishna, is the cause of all causes. And He is *adi-purusam*, the original person.

Dr. Daughtery: Are we to understand that you perceive in Krishna consciousness, in the Vedic scriptures, a fuller revelation of what it means to be a devotee of God, a revelation that preceded the Judaic-Christian tradition, and that this is why you now find it more meaningful?

Srila Bhaktipada: It's a question of developing the intensity of our love. In the Bible it is also stated, "God is love," but how do we further develop that loving relationship? It's by association, by getting to know each other. If a person is actually loveable, you will love him more as you know him better. Since God is the most loveable person, the more we know about Him, naturally the more we love Him.

The Vedic revelation is the most complete. In it, you will find thousands of God's names, elaborate descriptions of God's form, knowledge of God's pastimes—everything about Him. In the Bible, you will find a synopsis. For instance, Genesis states, "In the beginning, God created the heaven and the earth." That is a fact. But exactly how did He do it? In the Vedic scriptures you will find an exact scientific description of how that creation takes place. The knowledge is not contradictory; the difference is like that between a pocket dictionary and an unabridged one. There is no conflict, but one presents the information completely.

On the basis of Vedic knowledge, we can become free from all material entanglements. We can see God as He is—the most loveable person. And when our love has fully developed, we will have no problem giving up this material world. Our attachment to this world is due to our not knowing and loving Krishna.

If a child is holding onto something, and you want him to give it up, the best way is to offer him something different, something he wants more. Then he will drop whatever he was holding so tightly. This material world of birth, old age, disease, and death is not very relishable. As soon as we see its temporary nature, we immediately lose our attachment for it. We have to give it up in any case. But when we see the nature of Krishna—His eternal beauty and form—we at once become attached to Him. That is positive attraction, and that is better. There's no question of having both the material world and Krishna at the same time, however. As Christ said, you cannot simultaneously love God and mammon. Developing attachment to God means becoming automatically detached from matter.

Student: You mentioned that within the Judaic and Christian traditions, if one realizes that what it's all about is love of God, then that's a legitimate way of approaching God. But why was it that within your experience, within the Baptist tradition, you missed that sort of consciousness?

Srila Bhaktipada: Because there was no spiritual master within that tradition who could present it to me. You have to learn at the feet of one who knows. By Krishna's arrangement, I met a pure devotee of Krishna, His Divine Grace A. C. Bhaktivedanta Swami Prabhupada. Therefore I became Krishna's devotee.

Student: Is reality in our perception or in things in themselves?

Srila Bhaktipada: In *Bhagavad-gita*, Krishna defines reality: "Those who are seers of the truth have concluded that of the nonexistent there is no endurance, and of the existent there is no cessation." (Bg. 2.16) Therefore reality refers to that which is eternal. The happiness of sense perception is not eternal, but the happiness derived from serving Krishna is eternal.

Student: Then the reality is in the things in themselves?

Srila Bhaktipada: The reality is God. Actions performed without relationship to God are material. They are unreal. Actions performed in loving relationship with God are real and eternal.

Student: Immanuel Kant says that we can never know a thing in itself, but it seems that you're saying we can.

Srila Bhaktipada: We can know everything if we know Krishna because Krishna is the center of all existence. All things exist in Him; therefore in Him you will know all things. Suppose that on this side of the room is a mirror, and on the other side are many objects. When we look into the mirror, we see all of these objects, but they are unreal. They're real reflections, but they are not the real thing in itself. The real thing is over here, on the other side. In God we see the reality, but in material life we see the reflection.

Student: Are you saying that we can know God completely?

Srila Bhaktipada: Well, it's like knowing the ocean completely. You can take only a sample of the ocean. We can know God by His qualities, but we can never know the extent of God.

Student: But how to apply that in everyday life, while recognizing the fact that although we're a creation of God, we're still apart from Him? This to me creates some sense of doubt about the will of God. It leads me to a sense of faith in doing the will of God, but never knowing completely what that will is.

Srila Bhaktipada: Therefore Krishna is very kind. He comes personally, leaves His instructions in the form of scripture, and is present in His representative, the guru. The guru is also an incarnation of Krishna. He's not God, but an empowered agent of God. After all, God is within your heart and within the heart of every living entity. But as long as we have material desires, we cannot perceive Him. In that stage, we must take instructions from the external manifestations of God: the spiritual master and holy scripture.

Therefore Krishna says, *tad viddhi pranipatena pariprasnena sevaya.* "Approach a bona fide spiritual master and inquire from him. He will instruct you in the Absolute Truth." (Bg. 4.34) Truth is not a matter of speculation. There's no question of speculating about how to go to New York. I just can't set out anywhere, in any direction. I have to consult the road map. Nor can I buy any plane ticket to any place and think I'll end up in New York. No. I have to pay a set fare to go to the desired destination, and then I get on the right plane and go. In spiritual life, the same principle applies. You just can't do whatever damn thing you want and get the same results. That's not logical. Nor is it confirmed by Krishna in *Bhagavad-gita.* If one has all kinds of material desires and performs materially motivated worship, he gets a material result. But if one becomes a pure devotee, he can go to the Kingdom of God.

Student: I still don't understand the relationship between your theology and Indian culture, which obviously seems very important for your whole endeavor. I was talking to some Indian people who were recently here. They felt there isn't too much difference between what they have in India and what they find here, and I understand that this comes close to what you intend. Could you explain how you perceive the world of Indian culture and how you reconcile the emphasis on the cultural issue with what you previously said about the religious principle underlying the different forms of faith?

Srila Bhaktipada: First of all, we're not trying to adopt Indian culture. We're after Krishna conscious culture. We want a culture that makes us think of Krishna, that's all. We don't care whether it's Indian or American or whatever. Thinking of Krishna is what's important.

A policeman wears a uniform, but he's a policeman whether

he has on his uniform or not. In one sense, the uniform is not at all important, but when he wears it, people immediately identify him as a policeman. In this sense, the uniform is important. A devotee is not a devotee because he wears this cloth, but the cloth is helpful because it helps him remain Krishna conscious. It helps him to remember Krishna and understand "I'm supposed to be different from a nondevotee." God's people are always a chosen people, separate from materialists. Unfortunately, only a few respond to God's call. "Many are called, but few are chosen." (Matt 22.14)

We're not at all attached to any national culture, but we're creating an atmosphere that makes it easy to remember Krishna. That is the injunction of Rupa Goswami: "Things favorable to devotional service should be accepted, and things unfavorable should be rejected." Herein lies the parameter for all the rules and regulations of Krishna consciousness.

Dr. Cox: Well, yes, but that doesn't quite answer the question. I mean, it's not just vegetarian food that we're eating. It's Indian-style vegetarian food. It's not just a beautiful Krishna temple. It's an Indian architectural expression.

Srila Bhaktipada: Because this helps us to think of Krishna. When Krishna appeared five thousand years ago, He actually did appear in India.

Dr. Cox: So the fact that Krishna came to India and that His tradition is an Indian tradition makes it important to make this an Indian cultural package?

Srila Bhaktipada: The importance is the relationship to Krishna, not to India. For example, we read in *Bhagavad-gita* about the battle of Kurukshetra. We're not interested in Kurukshetra because it's a battlefield. We're interested in Kurukshetra because on that battlefield Krishna was personally present driving His devotee's chariot.

If you look at Prabhupada's Palace of Gold, for instance, you'll see that it's not strictly Indian architecture at all. There's a lot of Renaissance influence. But it creates this atmosphere of remembering Krishna, and therefore we accept it. We also use tape recorders and movie projectors. Why? Because they're useful for serving Krishna, for remembering Krishna. We're not trying to create an Indian environment or Indian culture. We select things to produce a Krishna conscious atmosphere.

Student: Do you distinguish between Indian culture and Vedic culture?

Srila Bhaktipada: Yes. Vedic culture is the culture arising out of this transcendental knowledge.

Student: Will you discuss that?

Srila Bhaktipada: You'll find a lot in Indian culture that we don't have anything to do with: for instance, the whole realm of demigod worship and all the mundane holidays connected with it. Also, the Indian system of caste by birth is not at all our system of *varnashrama-dharma*, the Vedic social system. The Vedic system is not based on birth but on individual qualification.

Dr. Cox: So it's a selective use of those elements in Indian culture which help you to remember Krishna?

Srila Bhaktipada: Exactly.

Dr. Cox: And if there are elements in the cultural ambiance or environment here that would be helpful, you would also incorporate them?

Srila Bhaktipada: Yes. Over and over in *Bhagavad-gita*, Krishna says, *man-mana bhava mad-bhaktah*. "Always think of Me." Whatever is useful for thinking of Krishna—that's what we want.

Dr. Cox: I'd like to raise one point that keeps coming up when I find myself in philosophical discussions with members of the Krishna Society. From what I've seen, it seems to me that the Krishna consciousness movement generally focuses upon the need for the individual to attain a form of purity or transcendental status, and doesn't hold out very much hope for the transformation of social or corporate structures in the historical world. But I think there are many of us here who think of ourselves as representing a tradition in the Jewish and Christian perspective in which we would hold out more hope for the action and presence of God in the redemption of corporate, historical structures of human existence, rather than a more individual notion of deliverance. I think that reflects an attitude toward the material which is in some ways different.

Let me illustrate by going back to a point you quoted from Jesus on not being able to love God and mammon at the same time. Your interpretation is that you can't love God and the material at the same time. The more accurate translations of the New Testament, the more recent ones, put it very bluntly and say that you can't love God and money at the same time. This is really what mammon is supposed to mean.

Now, money and matter are not the same. A very, very important point. Money is, in fact, in some ways, a denial and rejection of the possibilities and beauty and significance of the earth, of matter, of the material, the flesh. Money is an abstraction. It's a piece of paper, or a piece of silver or gold, that has no significance except as it's used for exchange purposes—usually for one's own selfish profit, although not always.

And the idea that money is a diversion from our love and care for the material world, our devotion to and affection for the material world, I think, is more what Jesus was driving at when he talking about God and mammon. That's especially in view of the constant use of material things as the central focus of devotion: bread, wine, the human body. Now, I don't want to provoke an argument here, but I wonder if this resonates in any way with your perspective on things. I'm one of those people who believe it's most useful in an interfaith discussion not to avoid differences of opinion.

Srila Bhaktipada: No, of course not. I think that you've put us a little too much in a niche though, because factually we don't say that society cannot be redeemed in a corporate way also But it has to come by changing the heart. There's no question of having a changed society without changed hearts. So therefore our movement is a movement for congregational chanting. This is actually meant to be a very wide movement, to affect the whole of society. In this, we are very optimistic, because it is Lord Chaitanya's prediction that for ten thousand years this congregational chanting will become dominant all over the world and usher in a worldwide social change that will affect all areas of corporate society.

Dr. Cox: This will come at the end of the age of Kali?

Srila Bhaktipada: No, it comes now.

Dr. Cox: During the age of Kali?

Srila Bhaktipada: Yes, for ten thousand years. After that, Kali resumes its dark descent.

And I'd like to make just one point about the passage about mammon and money. The meaning of money is control. That is, money is the means by which one lords it over matter. If you give up this idea of controlling matter, then you can use matter in God's service. Now, that is perfect. Therefore the Lord is correct in saying that you cannot love God and mammon. Money is the means by which the whole world is controlled. In the heart of the conditioned soul is the idea "Let me be the controller." This alienates us from God because God is the only real controller. When we surrender our control to Him and use matter in His service, it is no longer matter but spirit. The only difference between matter and spirit is its relationship to God. The proposition of our Society for Krishna consciousness is to spiritualize this whole material world. Then we will have the Kingdom of God. By definition, the Kingdom of God is "the place where God is king." If we make God king here, we will have the Kingdom of God here and now. Without God as king, there is no question of this being the Kingdom of God. First we have to recognize that God is king, and this means a change of heart. We have to give up our individual tendency to try to be the controller, to think, "I'm the king. I'm the lord of all I survey."

Dr. Cox: Yes. I like this exegesis better than the one I heard before. I very much like your elaborate interpretation.

CHAPTER FOURTEEN

Conversations With Christians
(2)

(A conversation with Russell Edmunds, Catholic Deacon, St. Mary's, and Professor of History, Penrith Technical College, New South Wales, Australia)

Mr. Edmunds: What is the position of God, and His relationship to Jesus Christ and Srila Prabhupada?

Srila Bhaktipada: Krishna is the supreme cause. From Him expand many Vishnu-tattvas, all part of the same energetic source, and *jiva-tattvas*, the infinitesimal living entities. Prabhupada and Jesus Christ are both *jiva-tattva*, but they're empowered by God for a great mission. In *Bhagavad-gita*, Krishna says, "Whenever and wherever there is a decline in religious practice and a predominant rise of irreligion—at that time I Myself descend." (Bg. 4.7) Krishna descends, either personally or by His empowered representatives. Jesus Christ was undoubtedly such an empowered representative. Srila Prabhupada was also, because the *Chaitanya-charitamrita* states that no one can spread Krishna consciousness all over the world, either as Christ or Srila Prabhupada did, without being especially empowered by God. They can also be called *jagad-guru*, universal teacher.

Mr. Edmunds: They're equivalent? *Jagad-guru*? I've never been very clear on that particular point. Devotees usually refer to Christ in the context of a different *sampradaya* [disciplic succession]. Is that comment valid?

Srila Bhaktipada: Of course, Jesus Christ did not appear within the Vedic tradition. According to the Vedas, there are different instructions for men situated in the different modes

132

of nature: goodness, passion, and ignorance. Even the followers of goddess Kali, who are in the mode of ignorance, recognize a supreme God, although they are attached to worshipping the goddess for some material benefit. "Men of small intelligence worship the demigods, and their fruits are limited and temporary. Those who worship the demigods go to the planets of the demigods, but My devotees ultimately reach My supreme planet." (Bg. 7.23) Still, the Vedic process is so scientific and systematic that if they stay in the house of the Vedas, their elevation to the highest perfection is guaranteed. But a Christian has no such guarantee of guidance to the highest principle, and there is every chance that he may fall prey to speculative conclusions. Indeed, we find that there are hundreds of different Christian denominations, each claiming to be presenting Christian truth in its original purity.

Mr. Edmunds: Right, I see.

Srila Bhaktipada: Within the house of Veda, there are Vaishnavas—devotees of the Lord—and impersonalists. Amongst the Vaishnavas, there are four *sampradayas:* the Brahma *sampradaya*, which we are part of, the Shiva *sampradaya*, the Kumara *sampradaya*, and the Lakshmi *sampradaya*. They're all Vaishnavas, devotees of Krishna, the Supreme Personality of Godhead.

Mr. Edmunds: So, the basis of the genuine Vedic tradition has its antiquity, its genuine originality.

Srila Bhaktipada: It's original and complete. Prabhupada used to say that other scriptures may be compared to a pocket dictionary, whereas the Vedas are like the unabridged dictionary. For instance, the Bible says that God created heaven and earth, and certainly that is correct, but that is a summary. Exactly how God created is much more elaborately described in the Vedas.

Mr. Edmunds: Yes, it took me quite a long time to make the mental adjustment to that proposition. I think that a lot of Christians would have considerable difficulty understanding this, but if the perspective is historical, then it should be much easier to accept the authority of the Vedas, and the genesis of the religious conception. It would be interesting to relate that to the apparent revelations of God, especially in the Old Testament.

Srila Bhaktipada: Yes, and the reason is that God reveals Himself according to the capacity of the recipient.

Mr. Edmunds: And would this be the other side of the particular coin? The one side would be that the old Hebrew conception of God was very much determined by cultural limitations and historical experience, whereas the Vedic knowledge was direct cognition.

Srila Bhaktipada: You have to see it in terms of the evolution of the soul. It is the soul evolving gradually from the lower to the higher species. For instance, in the Old Testament, you find practically no elaboration or information on the soul. In fact, you can hardly find a belief in life hereafter. Generally, these topics are not dealt with, and certainly the eternal relationship of the living entity with God is not explained.

Mr. Edmunds: Yes, it's a very vague area.

Srila Bhaktipada: Very vague. The nature of the soul is not described. The Vedic literatures, which date back thousands and thousands of years even before Moses, however, contain complete knowledge of the soul, its transmigration in material life, and ultimately its relationship with God.

Mr. Edmunds: It's amazing. This perspective is a balanced perspective, and historical. A second question is one I have about early Christianity, especially in its efforts to understand the nature and the importance of Jesus. Early Christianity drew upon the philosophy and literary traditions of the time. The Hebrews did this, and others. Do you see Vaishnava theology helping Christians clarify the real meaning of Christianity for themselves?

Srila Bhaktipada: Yes, I certainly do. Dr. Harvey Cox, a very prominent Christian theologian of Harvard, has several times expressed that idea and has specifically mentioned his indebtedness to Prabhupada and the Krishna consciousness movement for opening up these perspectives to Christians by challenging them to have a deeper insight and experience in terms of their own religion.

Mr. Edmunds: Yes, I think this is the important thing.

Srila Bhaktipada: Prabhupada always said it's not what name you call God that's so important but the extent to which you've developed your love for God. If Christians actually became real Christians, they would be like Christ. St. Paul refers to Christ as the "firstfruits," (I Cor 15.20) which implies that others are to follow. But because Christians in general have wrongly understood the person of Christ, they say that He is the only son of God; therefore they neglect their obligation to become like Him, to be "perfect, even as your Father which is in heaven is perfect." (Matt 5.48)

Mr. Edmunds: They've made a formula of liberation.

Srila Bhaktipada: But actually the command is there to become like Christ, not in formula or word only, but in deed.

Mr. Edmunds: Yes, the perspective of Christ that we should have, according to the order of Christ, is to become like Him. This is my fundamental Christianity now, and I would like to be able to communicate this to my Christian Godbrothers. In a conversation with a Jesuit priest in Melbourne in 1975, Srila Prabhupada showed no interest in silence or silent meditation as an essential aspect of contentment in life. He said that Vaishnava meditation is transcendental activity. But the fact remains that silence is a major concern in the Russian and Greek Catholic tradition, and the practitioners feel a spirituality in that silence. What is the Vaishnava outlook on silent meditation?

Srila Bhaktipada: Real inner quiet, or inner contemplation, is achieved when one gives up sense gratification. One of the twenty-six qualifications of a devotee is silence, but this doesn't mean that he refrains from speaking. All the great devotees speak, but they never speak material nonsense, which is the cause of all problems. When we speak on the bodily platform, our words are nonsense, because we are not the body. But as soon as we chant the name of Krishna, we have complete peace. It is said that fear personified is afraid of Krishna. When Krishna's friends or devotees are in difficulty, they immediately cry out to Krishna, and their fear is immediately checked. This means that they immediately transcend the fearful situation and have perfect peace. This isn't due to silence in the material sense, but to the silencing of material desire and vibration. Their call to Krishna is completely transcendental.

Mr. Edmunds: This is probably what Prabhupada meant by saying, "What you call silence, we call transcendental vibration."

Srila Bhaktipada: Yes, that's in *Bhagavad-gita:* "One who sees inaction in action, and action in inaction, is intelligent among men." (Bg. 4.18) What does this mean? One may try to be materially silent, but his very attempt is an activity. That's action in inaction. He's trying to be inactive, but he can't be—not by sitting down, or trying to stop bodily activity. After all, he's doing something. Therefore, there must be reaction, either good or bad. And wherever there is reaction, there must be rebirth. Liberation from the cycle of birth and death is then impossible.

Mr. Edmunds: Because the senses are still there, there's activity.

Srila Bhaktipada: Whatever he's doing, it is still material; therefore it will produce a reaction. Even if you are physically still or silent, there's a reaction. Even if you refrain from sex, or even if you're elevated to the topmost material planet, there is a reaction, and you have to take birth again. For every material action, whether it's so-called good or bad, there's a reaction. That's the inherent quality of material action: a reaction follows.

On the other hand, a devotee who engages in all kinds of activities on Krishna's behalf is free from any reaction. For example, an honest teller at a bank handles millions of dollars a day, but the bank's profits and losses don't affect him. He knows that the money isn't his. But if he begins to think that the money is his and becomes an embezzler, then he is forced to suffer the reactions of his crime. Similarly, when we work for Krishna, the real proprietor of everything, and use everything in His service, not claiming anything as our own, we remain free from the reactions of material bondage.

It is always better to use something positively than to try to refrain from action. Of course, to do nothing is better than to do mischief, but positive action in a spirit of renunciation is the message of *Bhagavad-gita*. In the parable of the talents, Christ similarly pointed out the desirability of positive action. To different servants, various talents were given, and each used them according to his ability, and each was rewarded by the master. But the servant who hid his talent and didn't use it was condemned. He was unprofitable for his master, and even that which he had was taken away. We have to learn how to use everything in Krishna's service. Rupa Goswami says, "One who renounces things which could be used in the service of Krishna, under the pretext that such things are material, does not practice complete renunciation." (*Bhakti-rasamrita-sindhu* 1.2.256) Perfect renunciation is to work hard for Krishna without the slightest desire to enjoy some reward, material or spiritual.

Mr. Edmunds: This understanding of the contemplative way seems quite thorough.

Srila Bhaktipada: Furthermore, the realization resulting from this so-called silent contemplation is usually impersonal. If we want to come to full realization of the Personality of Godhead, we have to engage in devotional service. Krishna says, "Only by undivided devotional service can I be understood as I am." (Bg. 11.54) He is transcendental, and the method to attain Him is transcendental.

Mr. Edmunds: Yes, I must agree with that. On the part of the philosophical analogy involved, I must agree, because for eight years I practised transcendental meditation. In fact, I was a TM teacher.

Srila Bhaktipada: Such meditation can't take you beyond the impersonal realization of God, what we call Brahman realization.

Mr. Edmunds: The silence is empty. Space, the experience of space, is impersonal.

Srila Bhaktipada: It's actually a higher, more subtle form of sense gratification. Whether one wants to enjoy gross bodily sense pleasure, or to merge into the Supreme Enjoyer, his enjoying mentality is the same. Until we surrender to Krishna and agree to become His servant, there is no actual conversion, or revolution in consciousness.

Mr. Edmunds: Yes, exactly. I started to feel that way. At that time, I spoke to Srila Vishnupada. "You know," I said, "these days I don't even want to go on meditation weekends and extended meditation because I just get so lonely, so terribly lonely. I just want to get out of the place." And in the Christian tradition, Meister Eckhardt and others of the German school are very similar. What brought me real peace was chanting *japa*.

Srila Bhaktipada: Chanting produces real silence and consequently real peace. It's the ultimate meditation because it engages all of the senses in Krishna. Krishna is the sound engaging the tongue and ear, and mind in between. The object of all meditation is right there.

Mr. Edmunds: Yes, I've come to appreciate *japa*, along with the short practice of the Jesus prayer, and the literature. If only Christians could really discover the Jesus prayer and its practice! It's very close to what the Krishna devotees are doing. When a devotee neither enjoys nor renounces the senses but engages both in the service of the Lord, I interpret this, in terms that I know, as one-pointedness. Contemplation requires one-pointedness.

Srila Bhaktipada: Yes, and that single point is Krishna. We must give everything to Krishna.

Mr. Edmunds: That's good. One thing that interests me very much is the Vaishnava artistic tradition, or what I would call iconography. I received a Master's degree in religion, and my thesis was on liturgical language, religious sensibility, and the extent to which they coincide, or fail to coincide. At ISKCON temples, I've been looking and listening very closely, and I've developed certain perspectives on this. I'm sure there are Christians who would be very concerned to look closely at the liturgy of ISKCON. Now, I'm interested in this in relation to Srila Prabhupada's statement that the devotees' paintings are windows to the spiritual world. To what extent is the liturgy and the iconography in the temple actually structuring or following the conduct of religious experience?

Srila Bhaktipada: Just as the devotees' paintings are windows to the spiritual sky, there are also other direct channels to the spiritual world. This material energy, in which we are now living, is described as a great shell. Now, no one can break out, but the divine can break in. The avatar of God breaks through that shell and directs us to experience the spiritual world by means of various windows. When a devotee takes material elements—paint, wood, stone, or other ingredients—and engages them in Krishna's service, they lose their material opacity and become transparent. Then one can see the spiritual world through them. Similarly, when Krishna incarnates Himself in the form of wood or stone or metals, these materials become transparent. Matter has been transformed into spirit, or spiritual energy, and actually reveals Krishna. Krishna is absolute. He is the source of everything. Therefore He can transform spirit into matter, or matter into spirit. For Krishna, there is no difference.

Mr. Edmunds: But for a Christian, of course, it's different. For the orthodox Christian, there is considerable difficulty in accepting such a conception. As you were saying the other night, the relationship between spirit and matter is hardly developed in Christianity. Therefore when many Christians come to the temple, they are shocked.

Srila Bhaktipada: That is because they do not really understand the prohibition in their scripture about false gods and graven images.

Mr. Edmunds: Yes, it's a very superficial reaction to what they see. They immediately categorize it in terms of Old Testament culture.

Srila Bhaktipada: If you accept God as absolute, how can you say that He cannot incarnate in material form? That would be placing limitations upon Him. God is unlimited—omnipotent, omniscient, and omnipresent. Otherwise, what do you mean by God? If He is limited, who has limited Him?

Mr. Edmunds: And you can't say that matter cannot be spiritualized because both matter and spirit are different energy vibrations coming from Him.

Srila Bhaktipada: God can do anything. Since everything is God's creation, it must have the fundamental nature of spirit. God is the Supreme Spirit. I'm reminded of one occasion when Srila Prabhupada was walking down Second Avenue in New York. It was a slum neighborhood, and the wind was blowing garbage everywhere. It was what we would call an ugly scene. Anyway, one of the devotees commented about it, and Prabhupada said, "No, it is not ugly. If you could see it as Krishna sees it, you would see that it is very, very beautiful."

Mr. Edmunds: Yes, it's a matter of perception.

Srila Bhaktipada: For one who sees everything in connection with Krishna, everything is beautiful because Krishna is all beautiful.

Mr. Edmunds: Yes, this has tremendous implications for the Christian's theology of incarnation because Christians have the impression that the Hare Krishna devotees see all matter as evil. Of course, this isn't true at all.

Srila Bhaktipada: We see everything disconnected from Krishna as ugly and evil. But matter connected to Krishna is beautiful and good.

Mr. Edmunds: Yes, it's transformed. If this can be effectively communicated to Christians, I think it would be a big breakthrough.

Srila Bhaktipada: *Om purnam adah purnam idam.* Everything is perfect. Matter, or the objects of this world, become imperfect, or incomplete, only when they are disconnected from Krishna. For instance, as long as your hand is connected to your body, it is very useful and beautiful, but if it is severed, it is ugly and useless, although it may still be called a hand. Disconnecting anything from God is sin.

Mr. Edmunds: Sin can be defined as getting off the point, or off the target, as being deflected.

Srila Bhaktipada: In the New Testament, sin is defined as disobedience to the laws of God.

Mr. Edmunds: I've been reading a book by Bhaktivinode Thakura, in which he says, "Nature as it is before our eyes must explain the spirit, or else the truth will ever remain concealed. A man will never rise from his boyhood."

Srila Bhaktipada: Exactly. Everything is coming from Krishna. Everything is a little sample of Krishna. We're also little samples of Krishna, but we're not Krishna. We're fragments of Him. We can never know Krishna entirely by empiric analysis, but Krishna reveals Himself completely to His pure devotee.

Mr. Edmunds: If open-minded Christians would listen to this and understand, I can't see why there shouldn't be full and total communion.

Srila Bhaktipada: We're certainly ready.

Mr. Edmunds: In one sense I often feel very lonely in that I know of no other Christians who share my deeper experiences with Krishna. In fact, devotees have told me that Krishna has called me to be a pioneer. This helps, of course, but it does not always remove the very human aspect of my position. I would be so relieved to share with other Christians who have approached my degree of commitment, especially those with whom I might communicate by mail.

Srila Bhaktipada: Yes, but you should not think that you're alone. Our spiritual master is always with us, as are all the previous *acharyas*. And Krishna is always with us as the Supersoul in the heart. We are never alone. Loneliness is material consciousness.

Mr. Edmunds: Yes, I recognize that. I've a long way to go. Is there anything about *bhakti* in the Judaeo-Christian scriptures, as there is in the Vaishnava tradition? Or must Christianity learn about the higher levels of consciousness from Vaishnava spirituality?

Srila Bhaktipada: Yes, we have to learn from the Vaishnava Shastras. In other scriptures, the Personality of Godhead is not described, at least not elaborately described. Love exists only between persons, and therefore knowledge of God's personality is the basis on which our love is evoked. The more you know about a lovely person, the more you love him. The more you hear about God's greatness, the more you develop love for Him. The Christians may develop loving feelings in the master and servant relationship, but there is not much development of the attitudes of friendship, parental affection, and conjugal love.

Mr. Edmunds: Except in very, very rare cases.

Srila Bhaktipada: Yes. Generally, those people are considered heretics.

Mr. Edmunds: Well, it wouldn't be too ambitious for one to see ISKCON, at this point in history, as an instrument in God's hands for introducing a new dimension to Christianity.

Srila Bhaktipada: We hope so. Chaitanya Mahaprabhu came to introduce that dimension to every living entity.

Mr. Edmunds: It's quite a revelation.

Srila Bhaktipada: Nowhere else will you find the conjugal relationship with God described so explicitly.

Mr. Edmunds: Higher mystical raptures such as those experienced by St. Teresa, St. John of the Cross, and others appear to be rather generalized experiences, a focus of Vaishnava ecstasy. With regard to the doctrine of the immanent Christ, especially in the poor and the suffering, and its relationship to the mode of goodness, Jesus said, "As you have done it unto one of these, the least of my brethren, you have done it unto me." (Matt 25.45) Is there any equivalent of this in the Vaishnava tradition?

Srila Bhaktipada: We extend compassion, mercy, and kindness not only to human beings but to all species of life, because everyone is part and parcel of God. If Christians apply their charity and kindness to human beings and yet slaughter animals, they are being inconsistent. Such charity is imperfect. Krishna says that He is the Father of all living entities, not just human beings. Before we can practice perfect charity, we must understand the universality of Christ's statement.

Sometimes people misunderstand this statement also in another way. It is a great mistake to think that the poor man in the street is God. That is Mayavadi philosophy. The impersonalists speak of *daridya-Narayana,* or poor Narayana. But how can God be poor? He is full in all opulence. Are we to understand that God is the poor man and not the rich? God is in the heart of every living being, including a poor dog. But this isn't to say that the dog is God.

When we perform charity, we should do so in knowledge. Charity can be performed in three modes: goodness, passion, and ignorance. Krishna explains this in *Bhagavad-gita:* "Charity performed at an improper place and time and given to unworthy persons without respect and with contempt is charity in the mode of ignorance." (Bg. 17.22)

Mr. Edmunds: Who is an unworthy person?

Srila Bhaktipada: If you give money to a bum, he will buy liquor with the money. So you are not helping him. In fact, you become a partner in his sinful act. You're not doing him a favor; you're just making his condition worse. Moreover, you have become implicated in his act of ignorance. *Srimad-Bhagavatam* informs us that when a cow, or any animal, is slaughtered, a number of people are implicated: those who raise the animal, transport it, slaughter it, sell it, cook it, serve it, and eat it. They're all conspirators. Similarly, if you give charity, which is your energy, to the wrong person, and it's used improperly, you become implicated. By the same token, if you give charity to the right person, you share in its benediction. If you give charity to a devotee, and he uses the money in Krishna's service, you are also credited with rendering devotional service.

Mr. Edmunds: As I see it, the true Christian lives by faith, as does the devotee of Krishna. Obviously, there can't be two different varieties of faith. Faith is the greatest of all human qualities. It cannot be restricted. Therefore, to formally, or theologically, distinguish between Christ and Krishna, or between Yahweh and Krishna, or Allah and Krishna, doesn't make any sense at this level of spiritual experience. One theologian said that to rest with an ultimate pluralism at this high point is intolerable. So, I have to relate Christ to Krishna theologically. If one's faith goes to Christ, this same faith can go to Krishna. Faith recognizes faith, and one faithful devotee can give his faith to another. So faithful Christians will recognize the faith of the devotees of Krishna. Faith is the path to the spiritual world, and that path leads to the spirit of Christ, which is a universal spirit. It's leading me on. When I met the devotees, I sincerely felt that Christ had led me to them. In fact, they were further along the path than I was. Faith is openness, complete openness. Would you care to comment on this?

Srila Bhaktipada: Faith is the subject. It is openness and the evidence of things yet unseen. Faith is real, and faith has substance. You say that Christ gave you faith, but obviously that faith was not perfect because you hankered for something more. What Prabhupada gave you was faith and knowledge. That is perfect: faith and pure transcendental knowledge. That knowledge is generally not found in Christ as He is portrayed by the contemporary church. Christ Himself said, "I have yet many things to say unto you, but ye cannot bear them now." (John 16.12) There is a perfect sentiment of faith in Christianity, but the philosophy or knowledge by which God is known is not complete.

Mr. Edmunds: You're absolutely correct.

Srila Bhaktipada: And that is manifest in the fact that the Personality of Godhead is not fully described in the Bible.

Krishna is the complete manifestation of the Personality of Godhead, and in Krishna consciousness, full knowledge of Krishna is revealed.

Mr. Edmunds: Yes, I agree. But when we're talking with Christians, can't we have as our common ground this bridge— faith? Even if the knowledge is incomplete, we do have that faith.

Srila Bhaktipada: Yes. "But wilt thou know, O vain man, that faith without works is dead." (James 2.20) Religion means to obey the laws of God. We must make our faith concrete. If we are to have any dialogue with Christians, or Muslims, or any one, we all must first agree to abide by the laws of God. "Thou shalt not kill" is God's commandment to everyone. As long as the Christians continue to slaughter animals and eat them, the dialogue will be difficult.

Mr. Edmunds: Yes, I understand. That's also my concern. For open words, the consciousness has to be clear.

Srila Bhaktipada: We have to abide by the laws of God. Meat eating, illicit sex, intoxication, and gambling are the four pillars of sinful activity. There's no question of developing faith, or love of God, as long as we engage in these activities. The real dialogue begins when we all agree to give up sinning.

Mr. Edmunds: That's the groundwork.

Srila Bhaktipada: Yes. But unfortunately, around the world, even so-called religious people don't want to give up sinful activities. They make excuses. Although Christ said, "Be ye perfect, even as your Father in heaven is perfect," (Matt 5.48) they say, "We cannot become perfect, but we have contracted Jesus Christ to take away the consequences of all our sinful acts. Therefore we can go on sinning with no worry." That's a most perverted philosophy. In Hebrews, this is specifically condemned: "If they shall fall away, to renew them again unto repentance; seeing they crucify to themselves the Son of God afresh, and put him to an open shame." (Heb 6.6) Chanting also counteracts sinful reactions, but to commit sin on the strength of chanting the holy name is the greatest offense. One who goes on disobeying the orders of guru and Krishna is just slapping them in the face.

Mr. Edmunds: Those who talk of communicating across the traditions on the basis of faith, as you say, have to actually follow God.

Srila Bhaktipada: Yes. That faith has to be made practical. The word of God is practical. We can know God by His word, but if we don't accept the commandments of God, what is the question of having knowledge of Him?

Mr. Edmunds: There's no real way of avoiding strict adherence to the laws of God. So, you would not accept the proposition of a number of writers who suggest that the method of dialogue and its content across the traditions should be determined by what is actually happening during the encounter. Would this be inadequate?

Srila Bhaktipada: Such dialogues generally end up as so much impersonal hogwash. I don't know anything other than what I have learned from Srila Prabhupada. I don't know of any method better for a dialogue, or for preaching. His compassion for Christians, Jews, Muslims, or whomever was exhibited perfectly. He presented Krishna consciousness as it is, and because it is genuine, it will act. When Christ went to the temple of the Pharisees, He decried their worship, calling it an outward appearance, and empty ritual. It had no real substance. They preached religion, but not knowing the real principle of religion, they acted against the will of God. Similarly, most of the religious world today is simply formality. There is no realization of God, or surrender to the Personality of Godhead.

Mr. Edmunds: There's a great deal of theological speculation.

Srila Bhaktipada: That's what it is—speculation. Mental gymnastics, word jugglery, a waste of time.

Mr. Edmunds: So, if the laws of God are taught by the devotees, then those with real faith or vision will recognize it.

Srila Bhaktipada: Anyone who surrenders to the Lord and follows His instructions will understand. The real principle of religion is surrender. At the conclusion of *Bhagavad-gita*, Krishna says, "Abandon all varieties of religion and just surrender unto Me. I shall deliver you from all sinful reaction. Do not fear." (Bg. 18.66) Very simple. Even a child can understand.

Mr. Edmunds: Is a Vaishnava always a devotee? What about the Eucharist, or Christ's association?

Srila Bhaktipada: It is very hard for devotees to appreciate a ceremony that celebrates the death of the guru. Actually, devotees rarely even discuss the disappearance of the Lord from His earthly pastimes. It is too painful. We don't like to think of taking the blood or body of Christ. But Christ meant it to be a remembrance of His life and teaching. "This do in remembrance of me." (Luke 22.19) Christ Himself gave us the proper understanding when He said, "He that eateth my flesh, and drinketh my blood, dwelleth in me, and I in him. As the living Father hath sent me, and I live by the Father: so he that eateth me, even he shall live by me. This is that bread which came down from heaven: not as your fathers did eat manna, and are dead: he that eateth of this bread shall live for ever." (John 6.56-58) Obviously, eating His flesh means to live by and for Him only. It is the ultimate surrender. It is nothing material.

Mr. Edmunds: Spiritual food, spiritual drink.

Srila Bhaktipada: Yes, exactly. His instructions: Give up sinful life and develop love of God. That is real communion with God. One serves the spiritual master not by loud affirmations but by executing his order.

Mr. Edmunds: This must be so. Frankly, I couldn't really appreciate that passage until now. That attitude, that atmosphere, is all around you. For centuries there's been almost a cult about Jesus and His body.

Srila Bhaktipada: But it's a misunderstanding to consider the body of Christ to be material. "If you do not believe when I tell you of material things, how will you believe if I tell you of spiritual things?" (John 3.12) If we lack philosophy, we can't really understand the difference between matter and spirit, between body and soul, and we'll be confused about the difference between the Christ we see and the real Christ, whose body is spiritual.

Mr. Edmunds: I've come to see that now. But it wasn't in my training.

Srila Bhaktipada: No, because there is some confusion there. Philosophy without religion is mental speculation, but religion without philosophy is simply sentiment. The Bible does not very systematically differentiate between the body and the soul. Because of that deficiency, people marvel at Christ's death and resurrection. Actually, "For the soul there is never birth nor death." (Bg. 2.20)

Mr. Edmunds: It's a peculiar switch. Christ was so full of life. He talked of life.

Srila Bhaktipada: Christ told His disciples, "If any man will come after me, let him deny himself, and take up his cross, and follow me." (Matt 16.24) There's reference to death in Christ's statement, but it's a death to the old life. "Take up your cross and follow me." That's a new life. Similarly, we have to die by giving up our material consciousness of "I and mine" and be reborn by initiation into the spiritual family of a bona fide spiritual master. Death always refers to the material body and the bodily conception of life, not the soul. The soul is eternal and full of knowledge and bliss.

CHAPTER FIFTEEN

Conversations With Christians
(3)

(A conversation with three ministers of the United Church.)

Minister 1: Was there a time in Christianity when reincarnation was considered or accepted?

Srila Bhaktipada: Certainly. Reincarnation has been accepted by people in all cultures. Christ Himself never denied it. When He was present, there was some discussion about His previous birth. "Some say that thou art John the Baptist: some, Elias; and others, Jeremias, or one of the prophets." (Matt 16.14) This indicates reincarnation, doesn't it? It was only later, when Augustine and Aquinas began speculating, that Christianity officially rejected reincarnation, with regrettable consequences.

Minister 3: Where does Jesus fit into your doctrine?

Srila Bhaktipada: We accept Christ as the son of God.

Minister 3: An equal of Krishna?

Srila Bhaktipada: As the son of Krishna.

Minister 3: Could He be the reincarnation of Krishna?

Srila Bhaktipada: He is an incarnation of Krishna. Since God is the controller of material nature, He is not subject to the process of birth and rebirth, or reincarnation. His appearance in the material world is not like ours. He is not forced to come here. Man is born and dies. God appears and disappears. There's a difference.

Minister 2: Do you believe that we reincarnate until we reach a point where we become a complete deity?

Srila Bhaktipada: We can never become God, but we can become perfect servants of God. That is our real position.

149

Minister 2: Isn't perfection the ultimate end?

Srila Bhaktipada: Yes, but we're not the complete whole. We are a part.

Minister 2: Can we ever reach that stage?

Srila Bhaktipada: Yes, we can attain perfection. Christ said, "Be ye therefore perfect, even as your Father which is in heaven is perfect." (Matt 5.48) If we cannot become perfect, how can we return to the Kingdom of God? There is nothing imperfect in God's Kingdom. But becoming perfect means becoming godly, not becoming God.

Minister 1: But didn't Christ come here to be our savior?

Srila Bhaktipada: He came to teach us the way to perfection, but if you say it's not possible to be perfect, how can you fulfill His instructions? To show us the path of perfection, He gave His very life.

Minister 1: He came to fulfill God's law.

Srila Bhaktipada: Does that mean that you don't have to abide by God's law?

Minister 1: No. His law is to love God.

Srila Bhaktipada: Yes, but how do you love God? "If you love me, keep my commandments." (John 14.15) We cannot break God's laws and then claim that we love Him.

Minister 1: So, what are His commandments?

Srila Bhaktipada: Ten basic commandments were given to Moses, but Christ reinforced these, making them even stricter. For instance, He extended "Thou shalt not kill" to mean that we shouldn't even get angry. "But I say unto you, That whosoever is angry with his brother without a cause shall be in danger of the judgement." (Matt 5.22) Moses said, "No adultery," but Christ said: "Whosoever looketh on a woman to lust after her hath committed adultery with her already in his heart." (Matt 5.28) There is no instance in which Christ lessened or negated the law. Rather, He made the law more stringent, for He established it on the higher principle of love.

Minister 1: He was the fulfillment of the law Himself.

Srila Bhaktipada: He showed us how to fulfill the law by directing all our love to God. Unless we love God, we cannot fulfill His law. We cannot hear Christ's word and then continue to sin. "If they shall fall away, to renew them again unto repentance; seeing they crucify to themselves the Son of God afresh, and put him to an open shame." (Hebrews 6.6)

Minister 1: But in the same passage there's mention of the falling away from grace. Grace is a gift received.

Srila Bhaktipada: It is grace to help you to become sinless, not grace to continue sinning.

Minister 1: Grace is not earned; it's just given.

Srila Bhaktipada: But we have to take it. Grace comes to those who strive by right means, refraining from sin and perfecting their lives according to the word of God. St. Paul writes, "What shall we say then? Shall we continue in sin, that grace may abound? God forbid. How shall we, that are dead to sin, live any longer therein?" (Romans 6.1-2) If we are sinning, we do not yet have the grace of God.

Minister 2: What are your thoughts on the future war?

Srila Bhaktipada: It appears that almost all nations are getting ready for it.

Minister 2: Before the second coming of Christ, it's said that there will be a great Armageddon. How far away would you say that is?

Srila Bhaktipada: We're not in the business of predicting days and years, but it will be soon. When the horizon grows bright, we say that morning is near. Similarly, any fool can see that they are preparing for war. Whether it is ten or fifty years, to God it is very soon. God sees time differently. The important point is that we should be ready for death at any instant. Readiness means ready to face death, which for us is the real judgement: "It is appointed unto men once to die, but after this the judgement." (Heb 9.27) What is the use in worrying about some future holocaust? We may not even survive tonight's sleep. It is not death that is to be feared, but the judgement after death.

Minister 2: How does this correlate with reincarnation?

Srila Bhaktipada: It is appointed unto men to die, but actually we are not men. We are eternal spirit souls. "Man" refers to the soul's present apartment, the material body. That body, of course, must die and the body's inhabitant must be judged. According to our activities, we either take another birth, or, if we have perfected ourselves, go back to Godhead.

Minister 1: Earned perfection, you mean?

Srila Bhaktipada: Better to say "qualified." For instance, I cannot see the sun if I remain shut up in the house. I have to qualify myself by going outside, where the sun is shining. Similarly, God's mercy is given freely to everyone, but as long as we remain shut up in disobedience, we cannot receive it.

Minister 3: Who sets the standard for sin?

Srila Bhaktipada: God. The Bible defines sin as a transgression of God's law.

Minister 3: But where is it recorded? In the commandments?

Srila Bhaktipada: In every scripture. Christ said, "Thou shalt love the Lord thy God with all thy heart, and with all thy soul, and with all thy mind. This is the first and great commandment. And the second is like unto it: Thou shalt love thy neighbor as thyself. On these two commandments hang all the law and the prophets." (Matt 22.37-40)

Minister 3: There are many interpretations of love and obedience.

Srila Bhaktipada: Yes, and therefore everyone needs a spiritual master, the representative of God, who can show us in practice how to surrender to God.

Minister 3: And how do you recognize this master?

Srila Bhaktipada: He is the person most addicted to God. His only business is serving God.

Minister 3: What about serving man?

Srila Bhaktipada: By serving God, we automatically serve man. After all, man is part and parcel of God; they are not separate. If we know how to serve God, we'll know how best to serve man. Unless we know and serve God, our so-called service to man may be harmful, despite our good intentions.

Therefore, Christ said to love God first, then your neighbor.

Minister 3: Do you believe that there is a living teacher for everyone? If so, who?

Srila Bhaktipada: He is the one who can best explain God to you and inspire you to serve God. I personally found such a teacher in His Divine Grace A.C. Bhaktivedanta Swami Prabhupada.

Minister 3: But where did you go for that?

Srila Bhaktipada: He came to me. It is stated in the Shastras that when one is serious to serve God, God sends the spiritual master.

Minister 3: Right! And I also have been sent my spiritual master, but it is not a living master. I don't think we need to find a living master.

Srila Bhaktipada: Then why are you asking questions? When we meet the bona fide spiritual master, all our questions are answered. When we read a book, we may have many questions, but when we meet the author who wrote the book, all our questions are answered. Actually, God Himself is the real guru or master, but He appears in a living form in the person of His pure devotee for the benefit of the conditioned soul. In the *Chaitanya-charitamrita* (Madh. 19.151), it is stated that by the mercy of Krishna, one gets a bona fide spiritual master, and by the combined mercy of the spiritual master and Krishna, one gets pure devotion to God. The guru never says that he is God, but the confidential servitor of God. He is our living example of perfect God consciousness. Therefore we call him His Divine Grace. He is the mercy incarnation of the Lord.

Minister 2: What religion would you say you belong to?

Srila Bhaktipada: There are different religious faiths, but essential religion is one: *sanatan dharma*. Heat and light cannot be separated from fire, nor can *sanatan dharma*, real religion, be separated from the living entity. That dharma is service to God. Because it is our nature to serve, we are now forced to serve temporary material things. But if we serve God, the root of all existence, then our serving propensity becomes satisfied. When a tree's root is watered, all the leaves and branches are automatically nourished. Similarly, if we serve and satisfy God, the whole creation is served and satisfied.

Minister 1: Would you say that this is the greatest commandment?

Srila Bhaktipada: Yes. That is what Christ said.

Minister 1: Is there anything else greater? Any other commandment that has to be followed?

Srila Bhaktipada: All commandments are fulfilled in this.

Minister 2: Christians believe that you can't satisfy God. Christ is the only one who can satisfy Him for us.

Srila Bhaktipada: Then, if you satisfy Christ, will you satisfy God?

Minister 2: No.

Srila Bhaktipada: No? If Christ is satisfied, how is it God is not? Christ is God, isn't He?

Minister 2: Christ will satisfy us.

Srila Bhaktipada: But Christ said that He is satisfied when you obey His commandments. "He that hath my commandments, and keepeth them, he it is that loveth me: and he that loveth me shall be loved of my Father, and I will love him, and will manifest myself to him." (John 14.21)

Minister 2: But we can do that when He gives us His love.

Srila Bhaktipada: Christ has already given you His love. When was there a time when God did not love us? Was there ever such a time?

Minister 2: No, but we can be in a place where we don't comprehend that love.

Srila Bhaktipada: That's what I said before. And how do we comprehend His love? By keeping His commandments.

Minister 2: Only after we perceive love can we keep His commandments.

Srila Bhaktipada: God's love is always there, but you will not perceive it unless you keep His commandments. Why are some men perceiving God's love while others are not? Is it that

God gives His love to some and not to others? Is God partial?

Minister 2: He gives it to all, but we have the choice.

Srila Bhaktipada: Yes, and what is that choice? Whether to follow His instructions or not.

Minister 2: Whether or not to receive His love.

Srila Bhaktipada: What do you mean by "receive"? Receive is passive. Christ didn't tell us to just sit and receive. His message is a call to action, to render service to God. "Not every one that saith unto me, Lord, Lord, shall enter into the kingdom of heaven; but he that doeth the will of my Father which is in heaven." (Matt 7.21) And the apostle warns, "Faith without works is dead." (James 2.26)

Minister 2: We can't attempt to love God. Only He can love us.

Srila Bhaktipada: But it is due to His love that we can attempt to love Him. "We love Him because He first loved us." (I John 4.19) "Thou shalt love the Lord thy God with all thy heart, and with all thy soul, and with all thy mind." (Matt 22.3 7)

Minister 2: In response, only in response.

Srila Bhaktipada: Of course, His love is eternal. There was never a time when His love was not there. God is love.

Minister 1: You speak of becoming perfect, but the scriptures say that I was born in sin. I am a sinful person and will never be perfect.

Srila Bhaktipada: You, the soul, are never born. Only the body is born. But Christ commanded you, "Be ye therefore perfect, even as your Father which is in heaven is perfect." (Matt 5.48) Give up your bodily conception of life and come to the spiritual platform.

Minister 1: No matter what I do, there's no way I'm going to become perfect.

Srila Bhaktipada: If you think like that, you certainly never will. But if you don't become perfect, how can you go to the Kingdom of God? The Kingdom of God is perfect; nothing imperfect can enter there.

Minister 1: But "perfect" in the New Testament sense does not mean an attainment of perfection. It means receiving perfection. The Greek word for perfection is different. Love is perfect. Love can only be given. God is the source of love.

Srila Bhaktipada: My point is that God has already given His love. He has given Himself, and He is love.

Minister 1: And only when we receive it can we respond.

Srila Bhaktipada: You receive it by surrendering to God.

Minister 1: That's right.

Srila Bhaktipada: And what does surrender mean? It means that you give up your sinful activities. "If ye keep my commandments, ye shall abide in my love; even as I have kept my Father's commandments, and abide in His love." (John 15.10)

Minister 1: That's right.

Srila Bhaktipada: That's surrender. All conditioned souls want sense gratification. They want to go on sinning.

Minister 2: We are recognizing that we are sinful.

Srila Bhaktipada: Well, everyone recognizes that he is sinful.

Minister 1: I don't like the thought. I came up in a fairly strong Christian background, and I had to go to church and listen to somebody tell me that I'm a miserable, shivering, rotten sinner. Being a human being, I don't like hearing all that.

Minister 2: But that's what the scriptures say!

Srila Bhaktipada: Can't you understand that somehow or other in this material body you're always subject to suffering? Birth is suffering, old age is suffering, disease is suffering, and death is suffering. No one wants any of these things, but somehow or other we find ourselves in this suffering condition. Now, how to get out of this situation? How to stop suffering?

Minister 1: That's true. That I can understand.

Srila Bhaktipada: But we can stop all this suffering by God consciousness, Krishna consciousness. How is this? Because it brings us to the realization "I am not this body."

Minister 1: Even the most saved person, so to speak, still has trials and tribulations throughout his life.

Srila Bhaktipada: That's all right, but he should have the realization that he is not the body, that the soul is only in the body temporarily, like a driver in his automobile. When you arrive at your destination, you get out of your automobile, don't you? Similarly, at the end of this life, those who are in knowledge of God can get out of this body and never take birth again in this world. This realization will enable us to tolerate all the trials and tribulations we face in life.

Minister 1: Well, if you believe in reincarnation, you can say, "Well, if I don't do it now, I can do it later," when you get the next body.

Srila Bhaktipada: But you don't know what body you'll take next.

Minister 1: What do you mean?

Srila Bhaktipada: In physics there's a law: for every action, there's an equal and opposite reaction. Similarly, there's a spiritual law called karma. What you sow, you reap. If one lives sinfully, he has to reap the results of his sinful activities in his next life.

Minister 1: Some people think that if there's reincarnation— and I doubt there is—that they'll become a jackass in their next life. But I believe that if a man is to reincarnate, he'll be born in the body of a human.

Srila Bhaktipada: Not necessarily. If you live like a jackass, you'll get the body of a jackass. Nature doesn't waste its energy. For instance, if you don't move your arm for six months or a year, it will atrophy. Whatever is not used, nature takes away. Human beings are distinguished from animals by a more highly developed consciousness. After all, animals also eat, sleep, defend, and mate. But if that higher consciousness is not used, if a man simply eats, sleeps, defends, and mates like an animal, why should nature give him another human body? Nature is most economical. It is working under Krishna's directions.

Minister 1: There's a difference between the human and animal kingdoms.

Srila Bhaktipada: Yes, a difference in consciousness: the ability to inquire, "Who am I? Why am I here? Where am I going? What is God?" The animal cannot make such inquiries.

Minister 3: Then you believe that the soul doesn't retain the best of each incarnation, that after becoming human, it can go down again?

Srila Bhaktipada: If you misuse this human life, you can return to a lower species. Why not? Lord Krishna explains in *Bhagavad-gita*, "Whatever state of being one remembers when he quits his body, that state he will attain without fail." (Bg. 8.6)

Now, what one remembers at the time of death depends on how he lives. We remember what has become most dear to us. Therefore a devotee who has made the Supreme Lord the most dear object of his life, and who always chants His holy name, is sure to remember the Lord at that difficult time. Therefore he is guaranteed to go back home, back to Godhead, but if someone becomes attached to a life of animal sensuality and lives like a cat or dog, that consciousness will carry him to such a body for his next term of existence.

Minister 3: How do we know when we're stepping over the dividing line?

Srila Bhaktipada: When you disobey the laws of God, you have to suffer the results. The laws of God are not arbitrary. They are actually meant for our benefit, to show us the right way to live in order to enjoy eternal life.

Minister 3: Don't animals have their own state of perfection?

Srila Bhaktipada: They are involved in an an evolutionary process by which they gradually come to human life. There are 8,400,000 species of existence, progressing in a natural evolutionary development up to human life.

Minister 3: Right. But they don't go back.

Srila Bhaktipada: No. For animals, there is no question of good karma or bad karma. Animals are automatically promoted up the evolutionary ladder, but humans are different. The human life is a life of responsibility. For this reason there are regulations for human beings but not animals. The scriptures prescribe do's and don't's for mankind. The state passes laws that men must follow. You cannot cross the street when the light is red. This is meant for people, not dogs and cats. Animals simply follow nature's law by instinct; therefore, like children, they cannot be held accountable. But we can choose to obey or not, and thereby choose to go upward, or back down the evolutionary scale.

Minister 3: You can lose your soul, but I don't think you can go back down the ladder.

Srila Bhaktipada: No, you cannot lose your soul, but there is regression, and then the evolutionary process begins again. In any case, the soul is eternal and can never be eternally lost. If a son disobeys his father, will the father punish him forever? Is God so cruel? What would be the purpose? Punishment is for correction. If there is no possibility of correction, punishment would have no value.

Minister 3: Well, it seems that yours is a very severe God.

Srila Bhaktipada: How is that? If we say that God damns someone to hell forever, is that less severe? Actually, He is neither severe nor lenient. He is simply fulfilling our desires. If we want to engage in unlimited sexual activity, we get a body that is suited for unlimited sex, like that of a pigeon or a rabbit. If we want to eat just anything and everything, we may get the body of a hog. If this is what we want, nature supplies a body in which we can indulge ourselves to our full satisfaction without shame. Depending on the quality of our consciousness at the time of death, nature supplies a body. We determine our bodies by our desire, and God supplies them. In *Isopanishad*, it is stated, "God is supplying everyone's desires since time immemorial." (Iso 8) The whole material world is situated on desire. We have come into this material world due to our material desires.

Minister 2: I'm still not convinced of reincarnation.

Srila Bhaktipada: Unless you understand reincarnation, it's very difficult to understand why one child is born with good opportunities—wealth, intelligence, beauty, and so on—and another child is born into a very difficult situation—poverty, illiteracy, disease. Where is the justice? Everything is clear when we understand that each person is reaping the results of previous karma. Otherwise how can we say that God is just or impartial? God, the all-loving, all-knowing Father, knows what is needed for the welfare of each person. Sometimes, to cure a child of typhoid, the parents do not give him any solid food. To an outsider, it may appear that they are cruelly starving the child, but this is not the case. Similarly, God places us in different situations according to our past desires, and with a view to our further spiritual development.

Minister 1: What is your principle against eating meat?

Srila Bhaktipada: First of all, we should not inflict unnecessary pain upon other living entities. And second, food should be offered to God in sacrifice. Afterwards, we accept the remnants of the offered food, which we call *prasadam*, or God's mercy. In this way, eating becomes a spiritual act. When we cook our food, we think, "I want to offer this to the Lord." Of course, God doesn't need to eat. He doesn't become hungry in a material way, but He becomes hungry by the love of a devotee who wants to see Him eat. That is God's mercy: He responds according to the loving desire of the devotee. Because we prepare our food for the Lord and then take the remnants He leaves for us, our food is called *prasadam*, the Lord's mercy. It is actually spiritual because the Lord has partaken of it in His spiritual way. And, because the devotee is thinking only of the enjoyment of the Lord, he cooks only those things Krishna likes.

While on this earth, Krishna Himself kept and protected many, many cows, and is famous as Govinda, the friend of the cows. Indeed, Krishna doesn't like to inflict unnecessary pain on any living entity. After all, in *Bhagavad-gita*, He says that they are all His sons. Therefore we never offer Krishna any kind of animal flesh—be it meat, fish, or eggs.

Minister 2: Is the cow the only animal sacred to Krishna?

Srila Bhaktipada: Every living entity is sacred. Krishna is in everyone's heart—in the heart of the cow, the elephant, the ant, the dog, and the dog eater. Because the Lord resides in the body, the body is a temple and is therefore sacred. He is even within plants, within wheat and rice, but because we do have to eat something, God has alloted different things to different living entities. If the tiger kills to eat, he does not incur any sin, because that is his quota. But if we kill unnecessarily to eat, simply to please our taste, we incur sin. After all, we have been given the knowledge of good and evil, and the independence to choose.

Minister 1: Who's to judge the difference between killing cows or killing anything else?

Srila Bhaktipada: But doesn't every Christian believe that God is situated in everyone's heart as the witness of activities and the ultimate judge? If we go to a grocery store and see shelves filled with nice grains, fruits, and vegetables, but go instead to the meat rack and choose to become implicated in the murder of an innocent animal, then we're responsible. Now, if there is nothing else to eat, we can kill an animal and eat it to sustain our life. That is allowed. But in modern society this is not the case. As long as such nice alternatives are available in abundance, why should we slaughter poor, innocent animals? If we do not allow them to live in peace, why should God allow us to live in peace? The slaughterhouses of Dallas and Chicago are directly linked to the slaughterhouses of Korea and Vietnam, or wherever material nature dictates next.

Minister 1: I've heard that man eats meat mainly due to social customs, or conditioning. Does man incur sin if he really doesn't understand that he's not supposed to eat animals?

Srila Bhaktipada: Is a child burned when he puts his hand into fire? Will the fire say, "Oh, this is an innocent child. He doesn't know my nature. I won't burn him."? No. Nature is no respecter of persons. Nature's laws are set by God, and it's up to us to learn them if we don't want to get burned.

Furthermore, we are not innocent. God's word clearly says, "Thou shalt not kill." It is also written in our hearts. To inflict pain on others is always wrong. "Do unto others as you would have them do unto you" is universal truth. We are without excuse. We are simply blinded by lust, the desire for sense gratification. But when we surrender to Krishna and serve His lotus feet, we lose all our sinful desires and become pure in heart.

CHAPTER SIXTEEN

Conversations With Christians
(4)

(A conversation with members of the United Theological Seminary, Dayton, Ohio)

Question: What separates us in our thinking, in our working together?

Srila Bhaktipada: From my point of view, nothing.

Question: As Christians, why can't we accept you?

Srila Bhaktipada: Perhaps because you misunderstand the relationship of Christ to God. We accept Jesus Christ as the son of God. That's no problem. But when you say that He is the only son, our question is, If God is so unlimited and great, why can He have only one son? We see this as a great limitation on the Almighty Father. Even an ordinary human being can have ten or twenty sons. Why is God limited to only one?

You point out that Christ said, "I am the only begotten son of God," but that is a qualitative statement, not quantitative. Factually, each and every living entity has the potential of being an only begotten son of God. Everyone has a unique relationship with God, and at the highest point of realization, one feels that there is only the Lord and himself. When Krishna was dancing with the *gopis*, the cowherd girls of Vrindaban, He expanded Himself to dance with each *gopi*, and each *gopi* thought, "Krishna is dancing only with me." Similarly, when Lord Chaitanya Mahaprabhu danced before the Jagannatha cart, there were several kirtan parties in action, and He expanded Himself to dance in each and every party. Each group thought, "Chaitanya Mahaprabhu is dancing only with us."

That is the greatness of God: He expands Himself within the heart of every living being, and in that relationship of love, it is as if only the Lord and that one living entity existed. Lord Krishna says, "The pure devotee is always within the core of My heart, and I am always in the heart of the pure devotee. My devotee does not know anything else but Me, and I do not know anything else but him." (Bhag 9.4.68)

Those who have realized the truth will see that there is practically no difference between Krishna consciousness and Christ consciousness. Who will deny that the Bible teaches the supremacy of God? "In the beginning God created heaven and earth." The Vedic scriptures also teach God's supremacy: "O great one [Krishna], who stands above even Brahma. You are the original Master....O refuge of the universe, You are the invincible source, the cause of all causes, transcendental to this material manifestation." (Bg. 11.37)

Christian scriptures teach that the living entity should surrender to God, and the Vedic scriptures teach the same. Krishna says, "Give up all varieties of religion and just surrender to Me." (Bg. 18.66) And Christ said, "Thou shalt love the Lord thy God." (Matt 22.37) That means to surrender. If we understand that the major tenets are in agreement, then the minor points become insignificant. When Christ said to love God, He didn't say, "You must be baptized in this way, or that way." Love of God is the foundation of all true religion.

Question: Didn't He say "with all your heart, mind, and soul?"

Srila Bhaktipada: Yes. This means to want God completely and nothing else. The problem is that people want God and something else besides. You cannot love God and mammon. To love means to completely repose your affections in one person. It can not be divided. Therefore, love means love of God because He is the only object in whom we can repose all our affections. In the material world, there is no such thing as love, for nothing is altogether lovely; what goes under the banner of love is actually lust. Real love has nothing to do with the attraction between a man and a woman. The word "love" should be used only in relationship to God. Unless we are willing to sacrifice everything for the service of God, we cannot love God.

It is interesting to note that in the New Testament there are three different Greek words denoting different kinds of love. Eros refers to the attachment between man and woman; philadelphia refers to the feeling that exists between friends; and agape designates that highest emotion, which expresses complete surrender of the soul to God. Agape is what we are talking about, and that is what St. Paul meant when he said, "Though I speak with the tongues of men and angels, and have not love, I am become as sounding brass, or a tinkling cymbal. And though I have the gift of prophecy, and understand all mysteries, and all knowledge; and though I have all faith, so that I could remove mountains, and have no love, I am nothing. And though I bestow all my goods to feed the poor, and though I give my body to be burned, and have not love, it profiteth me nothing." (I Cor 13.1-3)

Question: It seems to me that the love shared between the members of this community is very special. What are your thoughts on this?

Srila Bhaktipada: That is because it is actually love for God. For instance, you may see devotees bowing down and offering obeisances to one another, but actually they are not bowing down to the body. The obeisances are being paid to the Personality of Godhead who is residing in the body of the devotee. With such consciousness, one can bow down even to an ant, for Krishna is within every living entity.

Question: What is your vision for New Vrindaban?

Srila Bhaktipada: My vision is that of a place of pilgrimage where people can be inspired to practice the principles of renunciation. It's not that everyone should come here to live, but if they can come here and have some realization of the joy and benefit of spiritual life—that will be our success. It's natural for people to want to take a vacation, to travel, to see something new and wonderful. It's always been like that. That feeling was expressed by Chaucer in the *Canterbury Tales*, and that tendency is not bad, if properly used. What we have in the *Canterbury Tales* is essentially the diary of a pilgrimage.

Formerly, when people travelled, they didn't go to a hellish place of sense gratification like Las Vegas or Disneyland. When you go to such a place, you spend all your hard-earned money, and take away nothing of value. What have you learned? What have you obtained? Has your life been truly enriched? No. Your mind has simply been diverted from its problems, and you have gained nothing of permanent value. You have simply wasted your time and money, and that's a great loss.

Now if you go to a genuine place of pilgrimage, you become inspired spiritually. You gain transcendental vision and realize that this temporary material world is not the all-in-all, that this material body is not the ultimate goal of existence. You become inspired to elevate yourself spiritually and realize that "Above this body, I am a spirit soul. My real business is to reestablish my relationship with God." There is great value in such a vacation. Such realizations are possible through association with saintly persons at places of pilgrimage.

Question: What is your feeling about using medicine, and what system do you think best?

Srila Bhaktipada: There are many systems: the Ayurvedic, the homeopathic, the holistic, as well as the widely followed Western allopathic system. Whatever system you use, what is the actual healing power? A good doctor sometimes gives the same medicine to two patients with the same disease. One patient lives, and the other dies. Why? Same doctor, same disease, same medicine, but the results are different. If Krishna sanctions the medicine, it heals; it not, if doesn't. *Aham ausadham.* Krishna says, "I am the healing herb." Who is the healer–The doctor, the medicine, or Krishna?

Question: But does Krishna heal more through one system than another? Does He sanction one?

Srila Bhaktipada: Sometimes He sanctions one, sometimes another. I've observed some people cured by the homeopathic method, some by the Ayurvedic, some by the holistic, and some by allopathic treatment. There isn't any one system by which everyone is healed. Have you ever seen a doctor who can cure everyone? I haven't. And even if one is healed for some time, he becomes ill again and eventually has to die. Jesus Christ healed many people, but where are they now? Lazarus was raised from the dead, but how much longer did he live? A week, a month, a year? Whatever the case, he's dead now. So what's the value of raising the dead or healing the temporary body? After all, sickness is also to some purpose. In a sermon, Edmund Massey once said, "The fear of disease is a happy restraint to men. If men were more healthy, there's a great chance they would be less righteous."

We put our faith in Krishna, not in some system of healing. If He wants, He can heal us. If He wants, He can take us back to Godhead. We don't discourage a devotee from taking help from a doctor, or an electrician, or a plumber. What is the difference? They all deal with some material science.

Question: Then it doesn't show any lack of faith in Krishna to use certain medicines?

Srila Bhaktipada: Well, if a person becomes obsessed in search of health and spends all his energy trying to save the material body, he certainly becomes entangled. The real point is that ultimately, with or without medicine, we have to surrender to Krishna. Nothing is effective without Krishna. To take the help of a doctor is not to defy Krishna. After all, Krishna says that this material nature is working under His direction. The doctor is part of that nature, not above it. We are all servants of Krishna.

Question: So one way is not better than the others?

Srila Bhaktipada: What is better is that the devotee depends on Krishna. Take whatever help Krishna sends, and be thankful to Him.

Question: Can the women of your community come to see you?

Srila Bhaktipada: Not without an escort. I'm in the renounced order of life, and my association with women is always restricted.

Question: Don't they feel awkward that they can't come to see you?

Srila Bhaktipada: No. They can come at certain times, but not unescorted. If I'm here alone, a woman cannot come in. One has to understand the principle of celibacy. One can never be liberated unless he understands that the cause of material entanglement is sex. The prerequisite for liberation is detachment from sex. Therefore in Vedic culture, the interaction between man and woman is clearly regulated. Otherwise, there is a strong natural tendency for boys and girls to associate and engage in sex.

There is a saying that women are like fire, and men are like butter. When the two are together, the result is sure. Of course, you may ask, "What is the harm?" The harm is that the more one is attracted to sex, the more he becomes attached to this body; and the more one is attached to this body, the more he thinks that this body and its pleasures are the goal of life. Therefore, if one is serious about spiritual advancement, sex must be controlled.

The Vedas prescribe that a boy should be trained up in the principle of *brahmacharya,* celibacy. After rigidly following this discipline, he is allowed to marry. Krishna consciousness is not opposed to marriage, but it is opposed to illicit sex.

Somehow or other we have to get out of this material world. It is a miserable place of birth and death. Don't be fooled by the sugar coating of material nature. Be intelligent and use this life for developing Krishna consciousness.

CHAPTER SEVENTEEN

Conversations With Christians
(5)

(A conversation with Blake Michaels, Methodist Minister and Professor, Ohio Wesleyan; and the Ministerial Association of Moundsville, West Virginia)

Rev. Michaels: Much of Christian symbolism surrounding the infant Jesus uses an understandable human symbol, a little child, to evoke from us ordinary emotions and then translate or ennoble those emotions into a theological sphere...so we can see the religious meaning behind very ordinary symbols. This is another kind of portrait that emerges of Krishna in the literature—the child Krishna.

Srila Bhaktipada: We can reciprocate with God just as if He were our own child. In the Christian tradition, Mary had the Lord as her son. But this should not be considered symbolic. These relationships with God—as friend, parent, servant, lover—are real. Our material relationships with others in these roles is what is unreal. It is the eternal relationship that is real, not the temporary one. Our relationships with God are real because they exist eternally in Him. Indeed, we can relate as friends, parents, or lovers in this world only because these relationships exist originally in God. Developing our Krishna consciousness means to invoke again our loving relationship with God.

God is not an impersonal force. Although He is certainly far away for those who have no eyes to see Him, He is very close to a devotee. He is right here. The goal of human life is to know God as the Supreme Person. God is a Person, and we are also persons; therefore there's a personal relationship.

Minister: What is the relationship between Jehovah, God, and Vishnu?

Srila Bhaktipada: God is God. Our definition of God is found in *Brahma-samhita:*

> *isvarah paramah krsnah*
> *sac-cid-ananda-vigrahah*
> *anadhir adir govindah*
> *sarva-karana-karanam*

"Krishna, who is known as Govinda, is the Supreme Godhead. He has an eternal, blissful, spiritual body. He is the origin of all. He has no other origin, and He is the prime cause of all causes."

If, in your scripture, you refer to the cause of all causes as Jehovah, then Jehovah is another name for God. God is one; He cannot be two. God is the original cause of everything. But if you understand God just to be a creator, then that is different. There are many creators. In itself, creating is not sufficient qualification to be the Supreme Personality of Godhead. Even we create. Lord Brahma, who creates this material universe, is certainly a very powerful living entity, a great demigod, but he is not the Supreme Lord. Therefore we define the Supreme Personality of Godhead as the cause of all causes, *adi-purusam*, the original Person, the source of all that be.

Rev. Michaels: I more or less concur in that answer. Personally, I am of the conviction that God speaks through the Hindu tradition as well as through the Christian tradition. Both speak of the Lord as personal: a God of anger, and a God of love, a God of judgement, and a God of mercy, but in all senses an active God who controls, who has a purpose, and who in one way or another is bringing about His purpose. The Christian tradition rejects the purely philosophical formulations of the Greek tradition, just as the Krishna religion rejects the impersonalist philosophical tradition of India.

Srila Bhaktipada: There's a great similarity between the Vedic view and the orthodox Christian view of man's position in this world. That is, God's creation is perfect. Everything is coming from the all-perfect God; everything He does is perfect. That is Eden, paradise, the spiritual sky. Then there is a fall due to misuse of independence. After the fall, you can no longer say that this is a perfect world. As soon as maya or sin enters, there is imperfection. Maya, or illusion, is due to forgetfulness of God. The world will remain imperfect until we remember God or come to God consciousness by surrender to the Almighty Lord.

But why stay in this place where so many people are antagonistic to God? Rebellion against God has made this a horrible place. By surrendering to God, we can get out of here. The Kingdom of God is there, and the Lord is there inviting us to come back to His association. The Kingdom of God is perfect, eternal, full of knowledge and bliss. So why stay here? This material world is like a prison, where everyone, due to sin, is forced to suffer birth, old age, disease, and death. No matter how much we try to improve the prison, it is still an undesirable situation. No one wants to go to prison, but when we break the law, we are forced to go there and suffer.

Minister: The analogy of the prison is interesting. From the prison, one wants to escape. But as Christians we believe that this prison will be reformed. We wouldn't want to escape from the prison, but we'd give our whole life to reforming the prison and celebrating the fact that new life with freedom is coming. That is, the Lord will return, and this prison will be reformed.

Srila Bhaktipada: If you go over to the prison [Moundsville State Penitentiary] and ask the prisoners, "Would you prefer to have a better prison or to be free?" what would their answer be? Which is better? To move from a third class cell to a first class cell, or to move out the prison altogether?

Minister: The fact remains that we're going to remain in this prison, and we have to reform it.

Srila Bhaktipada: But Christ says, "My kingdom is not of this world." (John 18.36) Why do you want to stay here? God is calling us back home, back to Godhead. Remember the story of the prodigal son? The son left home and went into a far country, where he squandered all his father's resources and forgot his good father. But the father never forgot the son. He was always waiting and watching for his son to come home. And when the boy finally turned toward home, even while a long distance off, the father went running to greet him. God is so kind. He is just waiting for us to turn our attention toward Him and head home. Why should we stay in this place of birth and death when in our Father's house there are many mansions waiting for us?

Minister: We are not of the world, but we work within it.

Srila Bhaktipada: But what is our work? It's to get people to go back to the Kingdom of God. It's not to make this world a nice place to live in. That's impossible. "From the highest planet in the material world down to the lowest, all are places of misery wherein repeated birth and death take place. But one who attains to My abode never takes birth again." (Bg. 8.16) So how can we hope to reform this place if Krishna Himself calls it a place of misery?

Minister: But you haven't forsaken the world.

Srila Bhaktipada: No. That is true. In the last ten years, the Krishna devotees distributed eighty million books of transcendental knowledge. Our mission is to inform people about their real relationship with God. It's not to build more hospitals or try to make the prison nice. On behalf of God, we are informing everyone of the Kingdom of God and how to get there.

Minister: I think we could probably build some hospitals here.

Srila Bhaktipada: That will automatically follow as a by-product of a complete Krishna conscious society. But our business as spiritual leaders is to preach eternal spiritual life, not open body shops.

Rev. Michaels: There's a different emphasis on behaving toward the world, yet behind it there's the same conviction of a higher reality that we're trying to serve.

Minister: Just what does the Hare Krishna movement give to our society?

Srila Bhaktipada: We are giving knowledge of God. It is our duty to provide the means by which people will always think of God, by our books, by our advertising, by our temples, by our occupations, or whatever. We have to mold our life so that we're always thinking of God. We become like what we think about and what we associate with. If we associate with a thief, we may also become a thief. If we associate with those whose lives are vulgar and undisciplined, we also become degraded. By thinking of God, we associate with Him, and by associating with Him, we become godly. God is not different from the thought of God because He is absolute. He is not different from His name, nor from His form, nor from His thought. Somehow or other, if we can encourage people to think of God constantly, they will become godly. Then everything else will follow. This earth can become like the Kingdom of God when everyone recognizes God as King. But unless they recognize Him as King, how can you have the Kingdom of God? Therefore the devotees work on His behalf here and now, and at the end of this life go back home, back to Godhead.

CHAPTER EIGHTEEN

Conversations With Christians
(6)

(A conversation held with philosophy students from Notre Dame University, South Bend, Indiana)

Student: What would you say is the major point of contention between Christians and Krishna consciousness?

Srila Bhaktipada: As I've often pointed out, there are no contradictions between the teachings of Christ and the teachings of Krishna. But differences arise when these teachings aren't followed. The Old Testament commands, "Thou shalt not kill," and Christ expanded this to mean that we should not even be angry with our brother. Because Christ extended the Judaic law, we say that He came to fulfill the law. Christ was the embodiment of love of God and compassion toward all living entities, but if you do not follow Him, how can you claim to be His disciple?

When asked, "What shall I do to inherit eternal life?" Christ said, "Thou knowest the commandments. Do not commit adultery. Do not kill. Do not steal. Do not bear false witness. Defraud not. Honor thy father and mother." (Mark 10.19) If you love someone, will you constantly disobey his orders? The Old Testament says, "Thou shalt not kill," and Christ said, "Thou shalt not even be angry." So why are you eating meat and maintaining slaughterhouses? Can you imagine Jesus Christ taking a knife and killing an animal, feasting on its flesh, and then preaching, "Do unto others as you would have them do unto you."? Or, "Blessed are the merciful, for they shall obtain mercy."? Doesn't that seem inconsistent?

If you make such mistakes in your philosophy, then your

whole system crumbles. When there's such a miscalculation, everything that follows will be faulty. If you don't follow God's most basic law in the Ten Commandments, "Thou shalt not kill," why speak of love of God? If your spiritual leaders eat meat and sanction slaughterhouses, how can they expect anyone to consider them humane, what to speak of godly?

Student: We believe that this commandment applies only to human beings, not to animals.

Srila Bhaktipada: This means that you do not understand the meaning of the word "kill." If the commandment referred only to human beings, it would say "murder." Why do you interpret this commandment to mean that kindness, justice, and mercy apply only to human beings and not to animals? According to the *Mahabharata*, a person who does not disturb or cause painful action in the mind of any living entity, who treats everyone just as a loving father treats his children, and whose heart is pure, certainly becomes favored by God.

Scriptures do not disagree. God does not contradict Himself. Or is it that God doesn't know how to communicate? "Thou shalt not kill" is a very clear statement, isn't it? If I tell you, "Thou shalt not kill," and you deliberately turn around and kill even an insect, what am I to think? We must follow the spirit of Christ and His disciples. St. Paul was so conscientious that he said, "If meat make my brother to offend, I will eat no flesh while the world standeth, lest I make my brother to offend." (I Cor 8.13) A devotee of Krishna can never support animal slaughter, nor give unnecessary pain to any living entity.

Student: Then why did Christ multiply the loaves and fishes? He could have multiplied fruits and vegetables instead.

Srila Bhaktipada: Jesus told His disciples to bring whatever food was there, and they said, "We have here but five loaves and two fishes." Christ simply multiplied what they had to feed the people so that they could stay to hear His message. But this doesn't mean He condoned animal slaughter. Now, if you find yourself in the desert with nothing to eat but a fish and a piece of bread, then you can eat it. You have no other choice. But when you have a modern supermarket filled with all kinds of fruits, grains, milk products and vegetables, you cannot eat meat without incurring sinful reaction, karma.

We have to understand the social context in which Christ was preaching. According to the Old Testament (Leviticus), a person offering an animal in sacrifice was allowed to consume part of that sacrifice. There are similar concessions in Hinduism. For instance, in Kali temples, goats are sacrificed on the night of the dark moon. Such sacrifices are permitted to give some facility to those who are addicted to eating flesh; instead of opening a slaughterhouse, they can kill a useless animal like a goat or chicken and offer it to the goddess Kali once a month. While the animal is being killed, a mantra is recited, reminding the meat-eater that in a future life, the roles will be reversed, that he will be eaten by the sacrificed animal. Therefore this whole process is to discourage animal slaughter and bring the meat-eater to question, "Why am I running such a risk just to eat a little flesh?"

Christ lived in a culture in which meat and fish were commonly eaten, and wine was drunk. Had He preached against such everyday practices, people would have immediately rejected Him. In order to save them, He had to make some compromises, just as a surgeon, to save a patient's life, might have to compromise a limb by amputation. That was His compassion for the ignorant masses. What Jesus and the Jews did at a particular place and time are not necessarily precedents for us. After all, the miracle of the loaves and fishes, or the turning of water into wine, are peripheral to Christ's central ethical teachings, found in the Sermon on the Mount. In that sermon, He preached mercy, purity of heart, and meekness, and said, "Be ye therefore perfect, even as your Father which is in heaven is perfect." (Matt 5.48) No one can listen to the spirit that pervades that sermon and at the same time sanction animal slaughter.

Student: But isn't the eating of plants also killing?

Srila Bhaktipada: Krishna says, "If one offers Me with love and devotion a leaf, a flower, fruit or water, I will accept it." (Bg. 9.26) We offer Krishna the kind of food He requests, and then we eat the remnants. In this way, no sin is incurred. God is *apapa-viddha:* sinful reactions do not apply to Him. He is like the sun, which is so powerful that it can purify even stool and urine. "The devotees of the Lord are released from all kinds of sins because they eat food which is offered first for sacrifice. Others, who prepare food for personal sense enjoyment, verily eat only sin." (Bg. 3.13) Devotees eat only *prasadam*, foods offered with love and devotion to the Lord. This means offering the Lord only what He wants. The devotees then take the remnants, so that they'll have strength to serve Him. In this way, they are always free from sin.

Student: Why can't Krishna give permission to eat meat?

Srila Bhaktipada: He does. He gives permission to dogs and tigers. If you study the teeth of carnivores, you will see that they are designed for tearing flesh from bones. But man does not have such teeth. Man's teeth are those of a vegetarian. His digestive system is also similar to that of the noncarnivores. In any case, a religious man does not kill and eat animals. If you want to do this, then God will give you an appropriate body, like that of a cat or wolf. Meat-eaters are awaiting such a future. After all, God is very kind. If you want to eat animals, He will give you full facility by awarding you a body with fangs and claws.

Student: Our sanction of meat eating is based on the viewpoint that animals do not have souls.

Srila Bhaktipada: And where do you get such information? You will not find it in the Old or New Testament. I challenge you to find me any passage in the Bible that says, "Animals do not have souls." You will never encounter this pernicious doctrine in bona fide scripture because the word of God is truth. But I'll tell you where you'll find it—in Aristotle, Thomas Aquinas, and Augustine. Aristotle based his views on personal speculation, and he was mistaken in so many ways, because, after all, he was just a living entity conditioned by imperfect senses. Aquinas followed in Aristotle's footsteps, and the Church unfortunately adopted Aquinas's views as dogma. Augustine simply wanted to justify killing animals and eating meat. You may follow the theories of such mental speculators if you like, but you'll not get the same results you'd get by following the teachings of Christ or Krishna.

Before saying that animals have no souls, we first have to understand what it is that indicates the soul's presence within the body. Obviously, we cannot see the soul, because the soul is nonmaterial. But we can know that the soul is present by its symptoms, just as we can know that the wind is blowing by the movement of the leaves on the trees. We cannot see the wind, but we can see its effects. Similarly, we have to see the effects of the soul.

Now, when a man dies, we say that his soul is gone. What is gone? The body is still there. It is still a bag of blood, pus, urine, stool—certain chemicals, in other words—but there is no consciousness. That's the thing. It is consciousness that is the symptom of the soul, and because there is consciousness, one eats, sleeps, defends, mates, has feelings, desires, and so on. Humans experience all of this, and so do animals. So what's the difference? Why do you say that man has a soul and the animal doesn't?

Student: But man's life is sacred because man is made in the image of God. His biological functions might resemble those of an animal, but we believe that the soul is a human soul.

Srila Bhaktipada: The material body is like a dress for the soul. There are 8,400,000 different types of dress, and within all of them there's a spirit soul. This soul is neither human, demigod, animal, aquatic, or whatever. The soul is an eternal fragment of God. "When a sensible man ceases to see different identities, which are due to different material bodies, he attains to the Brahman conception. Thus he sees that beings [souls] are expanded everywhere." (Bg. 13.31) Moreover, Krishna explains that all living beings, not just man, are His sons: "It should be understood that all species of life are made possible by birth in this material nature, and that I am the seed-giving father." (Bg. 14.4) Now, do you think that a father would give his intelligent son permission to kill and eat his less intelligent son?

Student: But animals aren't capable of making a philosophical search for truth.

Srila Bhaktipada: That's true. But little children can't either. Does that mean they have no soul? Actually, the consciousness of a small child is very much like that of an animal. Indeed, there are some animals that are more intelligent, and certainly more clever. But because you are mature men, and students of philosophy besides, you should make a philosophical search to find out the real nature of the soul. Go ahead with your research, experimentations, speculation, or whatever, but find out the difference between the living and the dead. This is systematically explained in *Bhagavad-gita*. "As the embodied soul continually passes, in this body, from boyhood to youth to old age, the soul similarly passes into another body at death. The self-realized soul is not bewildered by such a change." (Bg. 2.13)

The soul is transmigrating from one body to another right in front of us, but we need the eyes to see it. Why do people not understand? As human beings, you are supposed to be capable of higher thought. You should use your developed consciousness to understand the real difference between human and animal life. The difference is only in the development of consciousness. Even a tree has a soul, but its consciousness is undeveloped. When you go to kill an animal, the animal resists. It squeals loudly. How can you say that no consciousness is there? It may not be highly developed—a dog cannot read Plato—but you cannot deny his consciousness or his soul.

Consciousness, after all, is the symptom of the soul. When the soul is present in the body, the body is conscious; and when the soul is gone, the body is dead. All living things have souls, and are therefore sacred. All life is sacred, for it comes from the source of all life, God Himself. The soul is not less for being manifested in plants and animals, nor greater for being manifested in man.

The soul is great in all bodies because it is part and parcel of the Supremely Great. But we will never have this vision as long as we deny the unity of all in God, simply to allow ourselves the perverted freedom to kill for sense gratification. "If a man say, I love God, and hateth his brother, he is a liar: for he that loveth not his brother whom he hath seen, how can he love God whom he hath not seen?" (I John 4.20) If we want to see God in everything and everyone, we have to treat everything and everyone as we would God. This is the perfection of yoga and religion taught by Lord Krishna in *Bhagavad-gita:* "A true yogi observes Me in all beings, and also sees every being in Me. Indeed, the self-realized man sees Me everywhere. For one who sees Me everywhere and sees everything in Me, I am never lost, nor is he ever lost to Me." (Bg. 6.29-30)

This is the vision that brings universal peace and brotherhood. Hare Krishna!

ABOUT THE AUTHOR

Kirtanananda Swami Bhaktipada was born September 6, 1937, in Peekskill, New York. The son of a Baptist minister, he was imbued with the missionary spirit from earliest childhood: he would gather his playmates around him and preach to them. His parents took great care to teach him the values of Christianity, and he was a willing student.

In college, he joined the debating team, and showed great skill as a propounder of logical argument. Debate showed him that there are always two sides to any argument, and he began to wonder if spirituality could be limited to any one doctrine.

In 1958, he graduated from Maryville College, valedictorian and magna cum lauda. As a Woodrow Wilson Fellow, he worked toward his doctorate in American history at Columbia University. His thesis was entitled "Religious Revivalism in the Old South."

Setting aside his studies, he went to India in 1965 in search of a genuine spiritual master. His search was not fulfilled until his return to New York in 1966, when he met His Divine Grace, A.C. Bhaktivedanta Swami Prabhupada, the founder-acharya of the Hare Krishna movement. Here was the answer to his quest: spiritual life that transcended doctrinal concepts and led to pure love of God. He became Prabhupada's first American disciple, and, in 1968, founded the New Vrindaban community in West Virginia.

In 1977, Bhaktipada returned to India to see Prabhupada, who was about to leave this mortal world. Prabhupada requested him to carry on the discipular succession and become a spiritual master himself. Bhaktipada then returned to New Vrindaban, where he supervised the construction of Prabhupada's Palace of Gold.

Completed in 1979, the Palace—a memorial to Srila Prabhupada—has become a popular tourist attraction.

In 1985, Srila Bhaktipada inaugurated construction of the great Radha Krishna Temple of Understanding, destined to be the world's largest Krsna temple when completed in 1995. This ambitious architectural project has inspired both Indians and Americans and sparked international interest in the expanding New Vrindaban Community.

Srila Bhaktipada's special mission is to develop a "Land of Krishna" that will serve as a beacon of Krishna Consciousness for the world.